Bertolt Brecht: Plays, Poetry and Prose
Edited by JOHN WILLETT *and* RALPH MANHEIM

The Collected Plays
Volume Four Part Three

Brecht's Plays, Poetry and Prose
annotated and edited in hardback and paperback
by John Willett and Ralph Manheim

Collected Plays

Poetry

Prose

ALSO

           in preparation

The following plays are also available (in paperback only) in unannotated editions:

Bertolt Brecht Collected Plays

Volume Four Part Three

Edited by
John Willett
and Ralph Manheim

Fear and Misery of the Third Reich
Translated by John Willett
Señora Carrar's Rifles
Translated by Wolfgang Sauerlander

Methuen · London

First published simultaneously in hardback and paperback in 1983
by Methuen London Ltd, 11 New Fetter Lane, London EC4P 4EE,
by arrangement with Suhrkamp Verlag, Frankfurt am Main

This play is fully protected by copyright. All inquiries
concerning the rights for professional or amateur stage production
should be directed to the International Copyright Bureau Ltd,
26 Charing Cross Road, London WC2

ISBN 0 413 47240 X (Hardback)
     0 413 53250 X (Paperback)

Printed in Great Britain by
Redwood Burn Limited, Trowbridge

Contents

Introduction

In more than one way *Fear and Misery of the Third Reich* and *Señora Carrar's Rifles* occupy an exceptional place in Brecht's work. To start with, they were written not for the orthodox professional theatre but for semi-amateurs. Then they deal with contemporary political issues and make use – as his better-known parables do not – of contemporary characters and settings. They are also very short, the one-act *Carrar* in a sense being the longer, since *Fear and Misery* is really a collection of individual scenes, separately written with separate settings and casts. They make no use of such 'alienation' devices as subtitles, heightened speech or the breaking of the action by songs. Each is predominantly naturalistic to an extent quite unusual in Brecht's case, though the particular flavour of his writing is still impossible to disguise. And each admits the use of empathy – that identification of the actor with his role and of audience with actor which Brecht had previously ruled out. In *Carrar*'s case the change is openly declared by the note stating that this is 'Aristotelian (empathy-) drama'. With the *Fear and Misery* scenes it is more tacit, somewhat in the sense of a letter to their director Slatan Dudow where Brecht (in July 1937) confessed that he no longer wished to dismiss empathy altogether but rather to speak of its inconsistencies, of 'a crisis of empathy'. Taken together, these apparent shifts of position led a number of Communist critics at the time to see Brecht as something of a convert to the still new official aesthetic of Socialist Realism. And certainly the first five years of his exile saw him keener than either before or since to gear his work to urgent, immediate political tasks.

Prior to Hitler's assumption of power in 1933 Brecht had written less about the Nazis than we now tend to think. Even in his most sharply political plays (like *The Mother* and the film *Kuhle Wampe*) Fascism is not alluded to, while among the poems only the 'Song of the SA man' and 'When the fascists kept getting stronger' seem firmly to belong before that date. Like the KPD itself, Brecht had seen capitalism as the main enemy and the Nazis as merely the last of its hired supporters, too contemptible to be worth bothering about. Once Hitler was installed, however, and particularly following his own exile that March, he was far quicker than most of his political friends to grasp the realities of Nazi rule. Along with Koestler and Gustav Regler he took a hand in the preparation of the Brown Books which Willi Muenzenberg began issuing from Paris that summer – publications whose wealth of detail (however inadequately checked) about the repression in Hitler's new Third Reich was to be very relevant to *Fear and Misery* – while with Hanns Eisler he compiled the book of *Lieder Gedichte Chöre* published by Muenzenberg the following year. This contained twelve new anti-Nazi poems (six of them parodistic 'Hitler Chorales') and ended with the powerful 'Germany, pale mother' – about half of the poems in question can be found in *Poems 1913–1956* between pp. 206–219. Admittedly he had two major preoccupations at this point, neither of them originally inspired by Hitler's policies: these were the writing of *The Threepenny Novel* and the completion of that *Measure for Measure* adaptation which ended up as *The Round Heads and the Pointed Heads*. This pair of hangovers from the earlier period took up much of his time, both before and after his decision to settle in Denmark late in 1933. One of them also involved close collaboration with Eisler during much of the ensuing year, and from then right up to the composer's move to America some four years later the two friends were producing new poems, songs and cantatas directly geared to the German situation, like the 'Ballad of Marie Sanders, the Jew's whore' and the long 'Ballad on approving of the world' (*Poems 1913–1956*, pp. 251 and 196 respectively).

During that first year in his new Danish house, only some thirty-five miles away from the German coast, travellers and visitors kept Brecht closely in touch with developments at home. At the same time a series of changes took place in Moscow which not only affected all Communist policy towards the Nazis but had an important bearing on his and Eisler's immediate concerns. For within weeks of the Russians joining the League of Nations – Nazi Germany now having left – and the first moves towards a Popular Front in France, the Moscow-based International Organisation of Revolutionary Theatres (MORT) was broadened and put under Erwin Piscator, the Communist director who was Brecht's major theatrical ally during some twenty years. Under the MORT was an International Music Bureau which Eisler had helped to form; he was soon to become its president. Almost at once, then, Piscator was commissioning the two collaborators to write what he termed 'a good United Front song' for the new party line, which they provided in December 1934 along with a 'Saar Song' for the impending plebiscite in the Saar territory (about which Moscow's policy had also changed) and the great minor-key fighting song 'All of us or none'. Next, in January 1935, Piscator invited Brecht to a conference of theatre directors which he was planning for that spring in Moscow, and from then on it looked as if Brecht's interests in defeating the Nazis, promoting his own theatrical works and ideas and getting a footing in the USSR would all be able to coincide. Among the results of his two months' visit, we know, were the essay on Chinese acting and the first formulation of his doctrine of Alienation (*Verfremdung*), the meetings with other visitors such as Lee Strasberg and Joseph Losey, and an (unfulfilled) contract for the filming of *The Round Heads and The Pointed Heads*; he also spent a good deal of effort trying to get film work for Helene Weigel and discussing Piscator's projects for German-language theatre in the USSR. Equally important, if less substantiated, is the strong possibility that it was this trip that stimulated the little realistic sketches which were to grow into *Fear and Misery of the Third Reich*.

For Brecht in Moscow was looking not only for theoretical clarification (at a time when Stanislavskyan naturalism was rapidly gaining ground in both East and West) but also for political tasks in the anti-Nazi fight. Besides the KPD secretary Wilhelm Pieck, who made a speech introducing a 'Brecht evening' on 26 April, he there met two other members of the Comintern executive, Béla Kun and Vilis Knorin who was specifically responsible for German affairs. With these people, who were known also to Piscator, he seems to have discussed the situation in Germany and the contribution which he, as a writer, could make to the broadening opposition from outside. That spring and summer moreover Piscator was developing his own idea of producing a whole series of short anti-Nazi propaganda films, which could be made separately in different studios: one of these was to tell the (supposedly) true story of the wife of a high German civil servant, who had been sent his ashes after his execution by the Nazis along with a bill for the cremation expenses. This was exactly the sort of material which Brecht subsequently used in his sketches, and although Piscator's scheme never got off the ground it is worth noting the Pudovkin subsequently used five of those sketches in his wartime anti-Nazi film *Ubitsi vychod'at na dorogu* ('The murderers are on their way').

It is only now, in the 1980's, that these still tentative connections are beginning to emerge; and much will become clearer when the MORT archives are examined or when Piscator's pre-1936 papers come to light. But we know definitely that Brecht had already begun writing about some of the themes dealt with in the *Fear and*

Misery scenes, since not only 'The Neighbour' (p. 152) and the poem 'The Chalk Cross' (*Poems 1913–1956*, p. 226) but four other poems written in the months preceding his Moscow visit derive from just the same kind of real-life report as he was to exploit in the play. Two more poems (ibid., pp. 245 and 246) came from reportages by another communist writer, F. C. Weiskopf, one of them actually appearing in the German-language Moscow daily paper while Brecht was there. There are other poems too that relate fairly clearly to his meeting with Knorin (as reported by Piscator's deputy Bernhard Reich), notably the 'German Satires' for the so-called German Freedom Radio and the 'German War Primer' poems which were written during 1936 and made first into an unaccompanied choral work *Against War* by Eisler before getting their final form. Eisler himself meanwhile started work on the large-scale 'Concentration Camp Symphony' which achieved performance over twenty years later as his *Deutsche Symphonie*. It was also now that he and Brecht were given two official Soviet commissions: one from the Red Army for *The Horatii and the Curiatii* – last and strangest of the *Lehrstück* plays – and another from the State Music Publishers for a Lenin Requiem on the twentieth anniversary of the Revolution. In short there are, to say the least of it, a number of pointers suggesting that when Brecht returned from Moscow on 20 May 1935 he had a clear idea of the Comintern's need for a sequence of short, realistic anti-Nazi scenes, and of the kind of material on which they could be based.

*   *   *

Yet it was two years before any tangible results began to emerge, and during that time the nature of Brecht's expectations from the Soviet Union changed considerably. Partly this was because of the reaction against the modern movement in the arts there, which became evident early in 1936 with *Pravda*'s denunciations of Shostakovitch, Eisenstein and other outstanding Soviet 'formalists': denunciations echoed for the German emigration by Georg Lukács's critical articles, with their schoolmasterly dismissal of reportage, montage and other departures from nineteenth-century naturalism. Partly it was due to the dissolution that summer on security grounds of such international organisms as MORT and Mezhrabpom-Film, which led to the abandonment of all Piscator's plans and to Piscator's own decision to settle in Paris. Partly it was due to the wave of arrests consequent on the Great Purge, which began seriously affecting the Moscow Germans and their friends in the second half of 1936. Admittedly this was also the moment when Brecht for the first time acquired an official status in the USSR as one of the editors of the new literary magazine *Das Wort* (though he was soon enough disgruntled with it when he found how little real influence he was to have). In all other ways however his hopes of gaining a new outlet for his work and ideas, and a new platform for the acting talents of his wife, were decisively knocked on the head. Any chance of a Soviet production of *The Round Heads and the Pointed Heads*, or of work on any of Piscator's film plans, or of the establishment of a major German émigré theatre now disappeared; while as for the *Lenin Requiem*, although it was apparently handed in in time for the November 1937 celebrations it was neither published nor performed.

While the Soviet climate was thus changing, the hopes of the European Left were turning towards France and Spain. In France the new Popular Front policy gained an absolute majority in the May 1936 elections, sweeping Léon Blum into power and helping in spire the renaissance of the French cinema; in Spain the Franco revolt against a rather similar Communist-approved government led to the outbreak of the civil war that July. At least for a time it looked as if the task of bodies like MORT would be taken over by organisations based in Paris, and at first this, along with the impending World Exhibition in that city and the mounting movement against War and Fascism, formed the centre of Piscator's new concerns. Among the Paris theatre groups to be activated as a result was the émigré cabaret called 'Die Laterne', which was now strengthened by the arrival of Slatan Dudow, the Bulgarian director of *Kuhle Wampe* and *The Mother*, whom Brecht had more than once tried to help find permanent work. With Hitler and Mussolini soon giving signs of their intention to intervene in the Spanish war, Dudow wrote to Brecht in Denmark that September to ask for a short play in support of the Republican cause. This now took priority over the *Fear and Misery* concept, and Brecht instantly started collecting reports and pictures of the fighting, particularly on the northern front. For the moment admittedly he was caught up in the preparations for the Copenhagen première of *The Round Heads and the Pointed Heads*, but early in the New Year he got down to the writing, modelling his story on Synge's *Riders to the Sea*.

Generals over Bilbao, the new play's earliest title, became out of date after June 1937 when Franco took that city; so Brecht shifted its locale to the Mediterranean and renamed it *Señora Carrar's Rifles*. It was agreed that Helene Weigel would come from Denmark to act with the group, and Brecht also wanted the production coordinated with that of *The Threepenny Opera*, which Aufricht was once again planning to present in Paris. 'I imagine it being performed in a very simple style,' he wrote to Dudow.

> Three-dimensional figures against limewashed walls, with the various groupings very carefully composed as in a painting . . . just calm, considered realism.

It was just this comparatively conventional form of presentation that most satisfied the critic of the local émigré paper *Deutsche Volkszeitung* and, along with the play's topicality, allowed it to be taken up by Communist or Popular Front theatre groups in several countries. In addition there was the deep impression made by Weigel's performance in the title part, which led Brecht to hope that she might be invited to play it in Zurich and other professional German-language theatres. Thanks to this combination of factors, *Carrar* was a success, which was a good deal more than could be said of *The Round Heads and the Pointed Heads*. The result was that from now on the latter largely dropped out of Brecht's calculations, while Dudow's stock went up.

Thus it was Dudow to whom Brecht communicated the start of work on *Fear and Misery*, even before the *Carrar* rehearsals had begun. 'At present,' he told him in July 1937,

> I'm writing a series of little (ten-minute) plays 'Spiritual Upsurge of the German People Under the Nazi Regime'; these and the Spain play would fill an evening. Minimal cast. As you see, in this way I too am turning to small-scale forms.

In the event the *Carrar* evening was to be filled out by some Brecht songs performed by Weigel, along with a showing of René Clair's film *Le Dernier milliardaire*. But Brecht saw the new scenes as the best possible way of developing 'epic' acting further after his wife's *Carrar* performance, and he continued to turn them out during the months that followed. By October the series consisted of five – 'The Spy', 'The Jewish Wife', 'Justice', 'Occupational Disease' and 'The Chalk Cross' – under the overall title *Angst*; in November there were seven; by the following spring nineteen, now to be presented under the *Fear and Misery* title, with *German March-Past* as a possible alternative; finally six more by the end of April 1938, when Brecht said that he was stopping at the grand total of twenty-five. By then it was understood that Dudow would stage some of them with a cast including Helene Weigel. Brecht's main concern at this point was that the actors should not simply be drawn from 'Die Laterne', whose level seemed to him amateurish, but should if possible include Ernst Busch and Felix Bressart. Dudow's was rather that the play's cumulative effect was too depressing, to which Brecht replied that 'it's not for us to preach the need to fight back, we show the fight going on. The final *No* seems enough to me.'

As staged in the Salle d'Iéna on 21 May 1938 the play consisted of eight scenes only, presented under the title *99%* – an ironic reference to the popular support for Hitler at the elections of March 1936 – and ending (as in our text) with the plebiscite that had followed the annexation of Austria a bare two months before the premiére. The prologue ('The German March-Past') and the introductory verses to each scene were set to music by Paul Dessau; this setting, which has apparently not survived, represents Dessau's first involvement with Brecht. The simple scenery was by *Carrar*'s designer Heinz Lohmar, this time with costumes by Sylta Busse, who had previously been with one of the German theatre groups in the USSR. Brecht himself received no royalties, nor did the play's run appear to have exceeded the two performances originally planned. Nevertheless the production was greeted as a success, and not only because of what was generally agreed to be another outstanding performance by Helene Weigel. Thus Walter Benjamin, who at that time was close to Brecht and had a special understanding of his work, wrote in *Die Neue Weltbühne* that Brecht had turned aside from his experiments in 'epic theatre' out of consideration for such émigré groups and their audiences. These needed no specific aids to 'alienate' them from the events shown: the alienation was already there, thanks to their political experience, and this made the new balance of the artistic and the political in the new scenes epic indeed. Soaked in current actuality, he said, this unique play would be an enduring testimony for generations to come.

Carrar meanwhile was being widely performed throughout 1938 – not only in Copenhagen (as reflected in our notes pp. 161–66) but in Stockholm, Prague, New York (by the People's Theater in April) and San Francisco; likewise by Unity Theatre in London and other British cities. And it continued to be played by similar left-wing groups even after the fall of the Spanish Republic in March 1939, which prompted Brecht to provide the new prologue and epilogue printed on pp. 167–69. The *Fear and Misery* scenes were not so popular, though Pierre Abraham staged his own translation in various French cities and finally, following the German invasion of Poland, in Paris itself with settings by Frans Masereel. Berthold Viertel too included 'The Spy' in a mixed programme for the Free German League of Culture in London in May 1939, just when John Lehmann published it in *New Writing* along with an article on film by Viertel himself. Both Viertel and Abraham however were friends of Brecht's, and no doubt the problem for other potential directors was that, unlike *Carrar*, the play as a whole remained unpublished until the middle of the Second World War. Though several scenes appeared in *Das Wort* (winning somewhat patronising praise from Lukács, to Brecht's considerable irritation), the complete work's expected apperance as part of the collected Malik edition – under the title *Germany – an Atrocity Story* – was blocked when that edition's Czech printers were taken over by the Nazis. However, Brecht's own interest, to judge from his correspondence of the time, lay rather in the possibility of a production in New York, where Eisler had been working since January 1938 and Piscator went at the end of that year. Even before the première Brecht was writing to Piscator to this effect, and from then on he kept the idea in his friend's mind. There is no sign that he even considered trying for a Soviet production.

*   *   *

The story of *Fear and Misery of the Third Reich* in America is one of multiple refunctioning and transformation with a view to the major production which never occurred. It begins with the visit of the poet's American friend Ferdinand Reyher some five months after the Paris première, when Brecht, now wholly immersed in that profoundly different play *Life of Galileo*, met him in Copenhagen. This was just when Brecht had made up his mind to follow Eisler's and Piscator's examples and put in for an American visa himself, and as a result he and Reyher now began looking at his recent plays to see how far these could be used to establish him in the US. *Galileo* was certainly the most important, but the most promising in Reyher's eyes was *Fear and Misery*, which he persuaded Brecht to let him adapt with a view to what he termed 'an honest commercial production' based on his own skills as a Hollywood rewriter. This meant in the first place tying the original scenes together in a conventional three-act plot. To quote James K. Lyon's account, Reyher

> constructed a frame story involving a young man from the working class named Eric. As the play opens on the night of January 30, 1933, this young worker has been beaten by the SA. He is helped from the scene by the daughter of a Jew, and the two fall in love. They reappear together or individually in a number of scenes. Their relationship has the effect of tying together otherwise unrelated action and events . . .

A mutual friend with whom Reyher discussed his adaptation told Brecht that it 'has a good chance of being a "hit" on Broadway':

> The scene that he read to me was so American, and the plan for the play has been worked out in such a way that the most sentimental viewer would listen and be captivated.

Among the suggested titles for this version were *The Devil's Opera* and *The Devil's Sunday*. It was never produced, possibly because Brecht failed to sign the contract which Reyher sent him.

Once war had broken out in Europe nothing more was heard of this scheme, and the play then lay on the shelf until Brecht and his family arrived in California in July 1941. By then the Russians too were at war and criticism of the Nazis was no longer denied then by the Soviet–German pact. Promptly they published a thirteen-scene version of the play under the *Germany – an Atrocity Story* title, followed in 1942 by an English translation called (for the first time in public) *Fear and Misery of the Third Reich*. That same year, at Alma-Ata, Pudovkin filmed *The Murderers are on Their Way*, based on 'One Big Family', 'Winter Aid', 'The Chalk Cross', 'The Spy' and 'Job Creation'; though the result was never released, on the grounds (says Jay Leyda) that its depiction of the Germans was not savage enough. Brecht for his part straightway began once again trying to promote the play in the United States. To H. R. Hays, his first wholly American translator, he wrote that he should try to get hold of a script, since this seemed to offer the best prospects of all his work. To Piscator he proposed it as a teaching exercise for his expected attachment (never realised) to his old ally's Dramatic Workshop at the New School. His letter concluded 'Of course it would require collaboration. You yourself would have to collaborate. Please write me what you think.'

It was not till the summer of 1942 that any such schemes began to look serious. Then Berthold Viertel staged four of the original *Angst* scenes for an anti-Nazi group called Die Tribüne in the Fraternal Clubhouse in New York, while Max Reinhardt himself also thought of producing the play. This stimulated Brecht to devise a new wartime framework for the scenes, which he described in his journal as

> a kind of PRIVATE LIFE OF THE MASTER RACE. one could put on stage the classic blitzkrieg lorry containing the third reich's soldiers in their steel helmets bringing europe the new order, which the scenes proper would show operating in germany. the lorry would be treated in ballad style, to a barbaric

horst-wessel march [the Nazi anthem] simultaneously senti-
mental and disgusting.

Though Reinhardt's interest petered out along with his scheme
to take over a New York theatre, Brecht completed the framework
as set out in his note on pp. 132–37, and evidently passed the
result on to Piscator. For in the winter of 1942/43 Piscator was
already making plans to stage this version at the Dramatic Workshop's semi-professional Studio Theatre, in a translation which
Hays was commissioned to make. Once again the project fell
through, this time because Brecht allowed Eric Bentley simultaneously to translate the play in apparent competition with Hays.
Hays cried off and Bentley went ahead.

Then in the spring of 1945, with the war on the point of ending,
Piscator made what on the face of it should have been the most
serious of the various proposals for an American staging of the
play. This was for a production off Broadway under the sponsor-
ship of the CIO unions. Brecht, who had already licensed a first
performance of the new version by the university theatre at Ber-
keley, was prepared to agree, this time specifying his conditions as
'a *very* good cast' and an 'excellent performance'. The translation in
both cases was to be Bentley's, now equipped with a new scene, the
'Peat-Bog Soldiers', written in New York largely by Elisabeth
Hauptmann (who was to get 17 per cent of the royalties). Eisler
too was drawn in to compose the framework choruses, the original
interscene verses having been cut; these were restored in the published version that same year. The '*very* good cast' consisted of what
Brecht described as émigrés and Piscator pupils, the former including most notably the Bassermanns, an elderly couple of great
eminence in the German theatre who however had never established themselves on the English-language stage and were not to
do so now. Three weeks before the opening Brecht himself arrived
from California, immediately rejected the introductory scene which
Piscator wanted to add – a quasi-informal discussion of dictatorship
and democracy in the light of the German surrender on May 7/8 –
and threatened to withdraw the rights. Piscator thereupon resigned
and was replaced by Berthold Viertel, who had also been in the
market for the play earlier. The performance was beyond rescue –
according to Brecht the budget had only been $6000 – and it was
devastatingly panned by George Jean Nathan and other critics. 'A
terrible failure', Eisler later called it. 'Brecht wasn't unhappy, but
he was embarrassed.'

Somewhat confusingly, American critics even today refer to the

original play by the title of this wartime adaptation, which was
already outdated by the time of its performance. This is probably
because for nearly forty years it has been the only published text
available in English. In fact the play's whole history, as outlined
so far, has meant that Brecht in effect provided us with two distinct
works reflecting his relationships − both theatrical and political −
with two very different parts of the world. For we now have on
the one hand *The Private Life of the Master Race*, a quite closely
woven sequence of scenes in three acts presenting the early years
of the Nazi regime from the imagined point of view of a victorious
army which has been turned back at Stalingrad. This, though far
less crassly commercial than Reyher's *The Devil's Sunday*, was certainly devised with American professional production in view and
following discussion with Clifford Odets and other Hollywood
friends; the title itself smacks of American journalism, and even
though Brecht himself may have devised it he virtually never used
it in German. And then on the other hand we have the loose
assortment of scenes designed for German émigré performance −
part professional, part amateur often on the most cheese-paring
scale, from which the American version was itself adapted. This
do-it-yourself theatrical kit, whose German text − the standard one
in that language − was the source of 99%, *The Murderers are on
Their Way* and other topical selections, evolved more or less
directly from Comintern policy, vintage 1935 and was aimed
mainly at politically sympathetic audiences. While it may be rem-
oter from ourselves than *The Private Life*, both chronologically
and in terms of theatrical tradition, it is more modern in form and
very much closer to the events portrayed.

*   *   *

If the play's ambiguous career makes *Fear and Misery* something of a
puzzle for the modern director, particularly in the English-speaking
world, this is only secondary to the ambiguity of its original form. Particularly in Eastern Europe, critics have tended to link it with
Carrar as constituting Brecht's most 'Socialist Realist' works in the
old Stalinist sense: that is to say, naturalistic in form and immediately political in content. *Carrar* indeed, in the twenty years
following Brecht's return to Europe after the war, was his most
effective passport to acceptability in the Communist theatre; during
that time, as Claude Hill has pointed out, it had more than twice as
many performances in East Germany than any other of his plays,
while that country's cheap Reclam edition, starting with a printing
of 50,000 copies in 1961, had reprinted sixteen times by 1977.

But with *Fear and Misery of the Third Reich* the position – reflected in its much less frequent production – is rather different, because although the individual scenes are often naturalistic they are generally much terser and more sketch-like, while the overall construction is not naturalistic at all. Hence Brecht's comments when Lukács welcomed 'The Spy' on its publication in *Das Wort* 'as though I were a sinner entering the bosom of the Salvation Army':

> he has failed to notice the montage of 27 scenes and the fact that it is just a table of gests: the gest of keeping silent, of looking over one's shoulder, of being frightened and so on: gestics under dictatorship. . . . the montage which he so decries originated in dudow's letters asking for something for the little proletarian company in paris. it shows how it is the proletarian exiled theatre that keeps theatre going, at a time when in moscow the former leader of a berlin agitprop group, maxim vallentin, has gone over to the bourgeois theatre

– which is Brecht's heretical way of describing the officially-approved Stanislavsky method.

The 'epic' aspect of this play, in other words, can be seen not only in the coolness of the writing (by comparison with that of *Carrar*) but first and foremost in the stringing-together of the scenes on a long processional ballad, itself comparable with several other characteristic Brecht poems, ranging from 'The Legend of the Dead Soldier' (1918) to 'The Anachronistic Procession' (1947). The actual order of those scenes as printed is not conceived in terms of 'acts' or 'parts' but simply chronological: what moves them relentlessly past us, in any order one chooses, is the regular rhythm of the linking stanzas. Brecht himself suggested to Piscator in 1938 that he might stage them by interspersing documentary material – presumably projections – 'in the style of Goya's etchings on the Civil War'; but really the analogy with *The Disasters of the War* is much closer than that, because it is the scenes themselves that are the terrible images, which the stanzas seem to caption much as do Goya's chillingly laconic titles. 'The whole thing must be played straight through,' he wrote on another occasion, 'possibly beneath a forest of illuminated swastika flags, with a ballad interspersed.' Max Reinhardt for his part was reminded of Büchner's *Woyzeck*, evidently by the brevity of the scenes. Benjamin saw them as providing 'an entire repertoire for the stage' and thought that when published – something that he never lived to see – they would read like Karl Kraus's *The Last Days of Mankind*, that enormous film-like panorama of Austria in the First World War.

Unfortunately Brecht for some reason never directed a production himself, and it was only after his death that the Berliner Ensemble presented some half-dozen scenes in a slow-moving production by five of the younger directors. Since returning from America he seems to have seen the play no longer as a work to be staged in its own right but more as a necessary prelude to any performance of *The Resistible Rise of Arturo Ui* – that other, much more oblique and superficial critique of the Nazis which, unlike *Fear and Misery*, really had been written for the American stage and conceived in largely American terms, yet never was seen by an American audience while he lived. It was almost as if he felt that the earlier play presented the facts of Nazism while the later could only offer a mocking commentary unintelligible to those who had not yet faced them; and meanwhile was hesitant to produce either till more time had elapsed. Having seen neither Ernst Ginsberg's production of January 1947 (on a red platform with a minimal setting by Caspar Neher) nor the (East) Berlin production at the Deutsches Theater a year later, he was still perhaps inhibited by the failure of *The Private Life*, and after that had made no further attempt to update the original play. Yet there is a powerful account of the Basel production by the then thirty-five-year-old Max Frisch, who contrasted Brecht's reticent, low-level view of the Third Reich in the 1930s with Carl Zuckmayer's far more successful *The Devil's General* 'which has relieved so many of us. Brecht doesn't give this relief.'

A friend told me he felt that everything Brecht shows us here is more or less harmless by comparison with what came later. Perhaps this is its greatest strength: we know the results, what we are looking for is the beginnings.

Written several months before Frisch met Brecht, this is an extraordinarily perceptive verdict for the time. And it is even more clearly true today. For by now we have been stunned into insensibility by the continued fictional and semi-fictional regurgitation of 'the results', to a point where pornography starts to take over and neo-Fascists become almost flattered by the scale of the Nazi crimes. With the normal imagination no longer able to relate such things to our common humanity, use of the word 'Fascism' has largely degenerated into nonsense, while dangerously few are able to distinguish symptoms of real Fascism when they occur. We are in short in a situation where some understanding of 'the beginnings' of the great German tragedy are urgently needed if the all-important links between petty everyday actions and outsize human atrocities are not to escape our grasp. What Brecht can do for us here is to take us back to the pre-Auschwitz phase of Hitler's reign, when many in the West considered that the German dictator was leading his country out of chaos, and viewed any incidental excesses as excusable in the fight against Communism. This is a case where the wisdom of hindsight vastly strengthens a play, because unlike the audience of 1938 we *know* what all the small-scale sneaking, lying and creeping eventually led to; we have looked at the end of the story, just as Brecht's notion of epic theatre demands that we should. And so there is no suspense, only inexorable demonstration.

Today this can grip audiences as the contrived wartime version could not. All that needs changing in the original conception of the play is the prologue with its image of 'The German march-past', the parade of a nation going to war, and the title with its allusion to a Third Reich now barely known except to those steeped in the historical background. Other such technical terms may need explaining along the lines of the glossary on p. 172. As for the earlier objections by Dudow and others that Brecht's picture of low-level Nazi life is too depressing and not 'positive' enough, they can now be seen to be very wide of the mark, so wide indeed that the optimistic 'No!' of the final scene sounds to us like wishful thinking, inconsistent with Brecht's ruthlessly critical approach. It is this approach above all that has to be maintained, whatever the selection of scenes chosen, and it depends (as Brecht said) in the sharpness of the portrayal, which in turn is a function of the actors' abilities, and the momentum with which the scenes follow one another. Once this tightness and drive can be achieved the scenes will have the same qualities as Frisch saw in them; that is, they will seem not like reportage but like carefully observed and purposefully formed extracts from life; what the Swiss writer termed 'a revue for the memory'.

If mankind had a memory surely things would start to improve? We would either shoot ourselves or change. Brecht hopes the latter. Hence the sober way in which he speaks to us, without ever being carried away or taking refuge in that vagueness which often masquerades as poetry; his poetry is his seriousness, his love of mankind. And his beauty, I'd say, lies in the dignity of his approach.

It can be no minor or secondary work that inspires such a tribute as this from a fellow-artist. Nor can it be ephemeral so long as the death camps haunt our mind.

THE EDITORS

Fear and Misery of the Third Reich

24 scenes

Collaborator: M. STEFFIN

Translator: JOHN WILLETT

Characters

1 Two SS Officers

2 Man
Woman

3 SA man
Cook
Maidservant
Chauffeur
Worker

4 BRÜHL
DIEVENBACH
LOHMANN
Jehovah's Witness
SS man

5 SS man
Detainee
SS Officer

6 Judge
Inspector
Prosecutor
Usher
Maidservant
Senior Judge

7 Two patients
Surgeon
Sister
Three assistants
Nurses

8 Two scientists, X and Y

9 Woman
Husband

10 Maidservant
Man
Wife
Boy

11 Daughter
Mother

12 Student
Young worker
Group leader

13 Announcer
Two male workers
Woman worker
Gentleman
SA man

14 Woman
SA men
Child
Worker
Young woman

15 Man
Wife
Released man

16 Old woman
Two SA men

17 Two bakers

18 Farmer
Farmer's wife

19 Petit-bourgeois
Two women
Young fellow
Dairywoman
Butcher's wife

20 Dying man
Wife
Pastor

21 Five boys
Scharführer

22 Two boys

23 Neighbour
Man
Wife

24 Woman
Two workers

The German march-past

When He had ruled five years, and they informed us
That He who claimed to have been sent by God
Was ready for His promised war, the steelworks
Had forged tank, gun and warship, and there waited
Within His hangers aircraft in so great a number
That they, leaving the earth at His command
Would darken all the heavens, then we became determined
To see what sort of nation, formed from what sort of people
In what condition, what sort of thoughts thinking
He would be calling to His colours. We staged a march-past.

See, now they come towards us
A motley sights rewards us
Their banners go before.
To show how straight their course is
They carry crooked crosses
To double-cross the poor.

Some march along like dummies
Others crawl on their tummies
Towards the war He's planned.
One hears no lamentation
No murmurs of vexation
One only hears the band.

With wives and kids arriving
Five years they've been surviving.
Five more is more than they'll last.
A ramshackle collection
They parade for our inspection
As they come marching past.

One big family

> First the SS approaches.
> Blown up with beer and speeches
> They're in a kind of daze.
> Their aim is a People imperious
> Respected and powerful and serious –
> Above all, one that obeys.

The night of January 30th, 1933. Two SS officers lurching down the street.

THE FIRST: Top dogs, that's us. That torchlight procession, impressive, what? Broke one moment, next day running the government. Rags to riches in a single day.
They make water.

THE SECOND: And now it'll be a united nation. I'm expecting the German people to have an unprecedented moral revival.

THE FIRST: Wait till we've coaxed German Man out from among all those filthy subhumans. Hey, what part of Berlin is this? Not a flag showing.

THE SECOND: We've come the wrong way.

THE FIRST: A horrible sight.

THE SECOND: Lot of crooks round here.

THE FIRST: Think it could be dangerous?

THE SECOND: Decent comrades don't live in such slums.

THE FIRST: Not a light to be seen either.

THE SECOND: Nobody at home.

THE FIRST: That lot are. Catch them coming along to watch the birth of the Third Reich. We'd best cover our rear.
Staggering, they set off again, the first following the second.

THE FIRST: Isn't this the bit by the canal?

THE SECOND: Don't ask me.

THE FIRST: Over by the corner's where we cleaned up a bunch of Marxists. Afterwards they said it was a Catholic youth club. Pack of lies. Not one of them was wearing a collar.

THE SECOND: Think he'll really make us a united nation?

THE FIRST: He'll make anything.

He stops, freezes and listens. Somewhere a window has been opened.

THE SECOND: Wozzat?

He pushes forward the safety catch on his revolver. An old man in a nightshirt leans out of the window and is heard softly calling 'Emma, are you there?'

THE SECOND: That's them!

He rushes round like a maniac, and starts shooting in every direction.

THE FIRST *bellows:* Help!

Behind a window opposite the one where the old man is still standing a terrible cry is heard. Someone has been hit.

2

A case of betrayal

The next to appear are the traitors
Who've given away their neighbours.
They know that people know.
If only the street would forget them!
They could sleep if their conscience would let them
But there's so far still to go.

Breslau 1933. Lower middle-class flat. A man and a woman are standing by the door listening. They are very pale.

THE WOMAN: They've got to the ground floor.

THE MAN: Not quite.

THE WOMAN: They've smashed the banisters. He'd already passed out when they dragged him out of his flat.

THE MAN: I simply said the sound of foreign broadcasts didn't come from here.

THE WOMAN: That wasn't all you said.

THE MAN: I said nothing more than that.

THE WOMAN: Don't look at me that way. If you said nothing more, then you said nothing more.

THE MAN: That's the point.

THE WOMAN: Why not go round to the police and make a statement saying nobody called there on Saturday?
Pause.

THE MAN: Catch me going to the police. It was inhuman, the way they were treating him.

THE WOMAN: He asked for it. What's he want to meddle in politics for?

THE MAN: They didn't have to rip his jacket though. Our sort isn't that well off for clothes.

THE WOMAN: What's a jacket more or less?

THE MAN: They didn't have to rip it.

3

The chalk cross

> Here come the brown storm troopers
> That keen-eyed squad of snoopers
> To check where each man stands
> Their job's to put the boot in
> Then hang around saluting
> With bloodstained empty hands.

Berlin 1933. Kitchen of a gentleman's house. The SA man, the cook, the maidservant, the chauffeur.

THE MAIDSERVANT: Did they really only give you half an hour off?

THE SA MAN: Night exercise.

THE COOK: What are all these exercises about?

THE SA MAN: That's an official secret.

THE COOK: Is there a raid on?

THE SA MAN: Like to know, wouldn't you? None of you is going to find out from me. Wild horses wouldn't drag it from me.

THE MAIDSERVANT: So you got to go all the way out to Reinickendorf?

THE SA MAN: Reinickendorf or Rummelsburg or might be Lichtenfelde, why not eh?

THE MAIDSERVANT *somewhat confused:* Won't you have a bit to eat before going off?

THE SA MAN: If you twist my arm. Bring on the field kitchen.

The cook brings in a tray.

No, you don't catch us talking. Always take the enemy by surprise. Zoom in from an unexpected direction. Look at the way the Führer prepares one of his coups. Like trying to see through a brick wall. No way of telling beforehand. For all I know he can't even tell himself. And then wham! – like that. It's amazing what happens. That's what makes people so frightened of us. *He has tucked in his napkin. With knife and fork poised he inquires:* How about if the gentry suddenly pop in, Anna? Me sitting here with a mouth full of sauce. *Exaggerating as though his mouth was full:* Heil Hitler!

THE MAIDSERVANT: Oh, they'll ring for the car first, won't they, Mr Francke?

THE CHAUFFEUR: What d'you say? Oh, of course.

Pacified, the SA man starts turning his attention to the tray.

THE MAIDSERVANT *sitting down beside him:* Don't you feel tired?

THE SA MAN: Bet your life.

THE MAIDSERVANT: But you've got Friday off, haven't you?

THE SA MAN *nods:* If nothing crops up.

THE MAIDSERVANT: Listen. Getting your watch mended was four marks fifty.

THE SA MAN: A bloody scandal.

THE MAIDSERVANT: The watch itself only cost 12 marks.

THE SA MAN: Is that assistant at the hardware shop still as saucy as ever?

THE MAIDSERVANT: Christ alive.

THE SA MAN: You only got to tell me.

THE MAIDSERVANT: I tell you everything anyway. Wearing your new boots are you?

THE SA MAN *not interested:* Yes, what about it?

THE MAIDSERVANT: Minna, you seen Theo's new boots yet?

THE COOK: No.

THE MAIDSERVANT: Let's have a look, then. That's what they're giving them now.

The SA man, his mouth full, stretches out his leg to be inspected. Lovely, aren't they?

The SA man looks around, seeking something.

THE COOK: Something missing?

THE SA MAN: Bit dry here.

THE MAIDSERVANT: Like some beer, love? I'll get it.

She hurries out.

THE COOK: She'd run her legs off for you, Herr Theo.

THE SA MAN: Yeh, I always do okay. Wham, like that.

THE COOK: You men take a lot for granted, don't you?

THE SA MAN: That's what women want. *Seeing the cook lift a heavy pot.* What are you breaking your back for? Don't you bother, that's my job. *He carries the pot for her.*

THE COOK: That's real good of you. You're always finding things to do for me. Pity other people aren't so considerate. *With a look at the chauffeur.*

THE SA MAN: Don't have to make a song and dance of it. We're glad to help.

There's a knock at the kitchen door.

THE COOK: That'll be my brother. He's bringing a valve for the wireless. *She admits her brother, a worker.* My brother.

THE SA MAN AND THE CHAUFFEUR: Heil Hitler!

The worker mumblers something that could be taken for 'Heil Hitler' at a pinch.

THE COOK: Got the valve, have you?

THE WORKER: Yes.

THE COOK: Want to put it in right away?

The two go out.

THE SA MAN: What's that fellow do?

THE CHAUFFEUR: Out of a job.

THE SA MAN: Come here often?

THE CHAUFFEUR *shrugging his shoulders:* I'm not here that much.

THE SA MAN: Anyhow the old girl's a hundred per cent for Germany.

THE CHAUFFEUR: You bet.

THE SA MAN: But that wouldn't stop her brother being something quite different.

THE CHAUFFEUR: Got any definite reason to suspect him?

THE SA MAN: Me? No. Never. I never suspect anyone. You suspect somebody, see, and it's the same as being sure, almost. And then the fur will fly.

THE CHAUFFEUR *murmurs:* Wham, like that.

THE SA MAN: That's right. *Leaning back, with one eye shut:* Could you understand what he was mumbling? *He imitates the worker's greeting:* Might have been 'Heil Hitler'. Might not. Me and that lot's old pals.

He gives a resounding laugh. The cook and the worker return. She sets food before him.

THE COOK: My brother's that clever with the wireless. And yet he doesn't care a bit about listening to it. If I'd the time I'd always be putting it on. *To the worker:* And you've got more time than you know what to do with, Franz.

THE SA MAN: What's that? Got a wireless and never puts the thing on?

THE WORKER: Bit of music sometimes.

THE COOK: And to think he made himself that smashing set out of twice nothing.

THE SA MAN: How many valves you got then?

THE WORKER *with a challenging stare:* Four.

THE SA MAN: Well, well, no accounting for taste. *To Chauffeur:* Is there?

Maidservant comes back with the beer.

THE MAIDSERVANT: Ice cold.

THE SA MAN *putting his hand on hers in a friendly way:* You're puffed, girl. No call to rush like that, I wouldn't have minded waiting.

She pours the bottle out for him.

THE MAIDSERVANT: Doesn't matter. *Shakes hands with the worker:* Did you bring the valve? Fancy walking all that way here. *To the SA man:* He lives out in Moabit.

THE SA MAN: Hey, where's my beer got to? Somebody's drunk my beer. *To the chauffeur:* Was it you drunk my beer?

THE CHAUFFEUR: No, certainly not. What d'you say that for? Has your beer gone?

THE MAIDSERVANT: But I poured it out for you.

THE SA MAN *to the cook:* You swigged my beer, you did. *Gives a resounding laugh.* Keep your hair on. Little trick they teach you in our squad. How to knock back a beer without being seen or heard. *To the worker:* Did you want to say something?

THE WORKER: That trick's got whiskers.

THE SA MAN: Let's see how you do it then. *He pours him a beer from the bottle.*

THE WORKER: Right. Here I have one beer. *He raises his glass.* And now for the trick. *Calmly and appreciatively he drinks the beer.*

THE COOK: But we all saw you.

THE WORKER *wiping his mouth:* Did you? Then I must have done it wrong.

The chauffeur laughs aloud.

THE SA MAN: What's so funny about that?

THE WORKER: You couldn't have done it any different. How did you do it, then?

THE SA MAN: How can I show you when you've drunk up all my beer?

THE WORKER: Of course. That's right. You can't do that trick without beer. D'you know another trick? You people surely know more than one trick.

THE SA MAN: What d'you mean, 'you people'?

THE WORKER: You young fellows.

THE SA MAN: Oh.

THE MAIDSERVANT: But Theo, Mr Lincke was only joking.

THE WORKER *thinks he had better be conciliatory:* Don't mind, do you?

THE COOK: I'll get you another beer.

THE SA MAN: No call for that. I washed my food down all right.

THE COOK: Herr Theo can take a joke.

THE SA MAN *to the worker:* Why not sit down? We won't bite your head off.

The worker sits down.

Live and let live. And a joke now and then. Why not? Public opinion, that's the one thing we're really strict about.

THE COOK: A good thing you are.

THE WORKER: And how's public opinion these days?

THE SA MAN: Public opinion these days is fine. You with me there?

THE WORKER: Oh yes. It's just that nobody tells anyone what he thinks.

THE SA MAN: Nobody tells anyone? What d'you mean? They tell me all right.

THE WORKER: Really?

THE SA MAN: Well of course they're not going to come along and tell you all their thoughts. You go to them.

THE WORKER: Where?

THE SA MAN: To the public welfare for instance. In the mornings we'll be at the public welfare.

THE WORKER: That's right, now and again you hear somebody grumbling there.

THE SA MAN: You see?

THE WORKER: But that way all you can do is catch them once, then they know you. And after that they'll clam up again.

THE SA MAN: Why should they know me? Shall I show you why they don't? Interested in tricks, aren't you? No reason why I shouldn't show you one, we've got plenty. I always say if they only realised what a lot we've got up our sleeve, and how they'll never survive whatever happens, then perhaps they'd pack it in.

THE MAIDSERVANT: Go on, Theo, tell them how you do it.

THE SA MAN: Right. Let's suppose we're at the public welfare in the Münzstrasse. Let's say you – *looking at the worker* – are in the line ahead of me. But I got to make a few preparations first. *He goes out.*

THE WORKER *winking at the chauffeur:* So now we're getting a chance to see how they do it.

THE COOK: They're going to smell out all the Marxists because they got to be stopped disrupting everything.

THE WORKER: Is that it?

The SA man comes back.

THE SA MAN: I'd be in civvies of course. *To the worker:* OK, start grumbling.

THE WORKER: What about?

THE SA MAN: Go on, you've got something on your chest. Your lot always have.

THE WORKER: Me? No.

THE SA MAN: You're a tough guy, aren't you? Don't tell me you think everything's a hundred per cent.

THE WORKER: Why not?

THE SA MAN: All right, let's call it off. If you won't play the whole thing's off.

THE WORKER: All right then. I'll shoot my mouth off for you. These buggers keep you hanging about as if we'd all the time in the world. Two hours it took me to get here from Rummelsburg.

THE SA MAN: What the hell. Don't tell me the distance from Rummelsburg to the Münzstrasse is any further under Hitler than it was under that racketeering Republic. Come on, you can do better than that.

THE COOK: It's only play acting, Franz, we all know what you say won't be your real opinions.

THE MAIDSERVANT: Don't you see you're just acting a grumbler? Theo won't take it amiss, you can depend on it. He just wants to show us something.

THE WORKER: Right. In that case I'll say. The SA looks very fine, but I think it's shit. Give me the Marxists and the Jews.

THE COOK: Franz! Really!

THE MAIDSERVANT: How can you say that, Mr Lincke?

THE SA MAN *laughing:* For Christ sake! I'd just turn you over to the nearest cop. Not got much imagination, have you? Look, you've got to say something you might be able to wriggle out of. Sort of thing you'd hear in real life.

THE WORKER: All right, then you'll have to give me a hand and provoke me.

THE SA MAN: That went out years ago. Suppose I said 'Our Führer's the greatest man there's ever been, greater than Jesus Christ and Napoleon rolled into on,' all you'd say was 'You bet he is.' So I'd best take the other road and say: 'They're a big-mouthed lot. You know the one about Goebbels and the two fleas? Well, the two fleas had a bet who could get from one side of his mouth to the other quickest. The winner was the one went round the back of his head. It wasn't so far that way.

THE CHAUFFEUR: Ha.

All laugh.

THE SA MAN *to the worker:* Now it's your turn to make a crack.

THE WORKER: I can't cap a story like that bang off. Telling that joke wouldn't stop you being an informer.

THE MAIDSERVANT: He's right, Theo.

THE SA MAN: You're a right bunch of turds. Make me sick, you do. Not a bloody soul got the guts to open his mouth.

THE WORKER: Is that what you really think, or is it what you say at the public welfare?

THE SA MAN: I say it at the public welfare too.

THE WORKER: In that case what I say at the public welfare is Look before you leap. I'm a coward. I don't carry a gun.

THE SA MAN: Right, brother, if you're going to be so careful about looking, let me tell you you can look and look, then all of a sudden you're in the voluntary labour service.

THE WORKER: And if you don't look?

THE SA MAN: Then you'll be in it just the same. Sure. It's voluntary, see? Voluntary's good, don't you think?

THE WORKER: That's where it might be possible for some daring fellow to make a joke or two about the Voluntary Labour Service suppose both of you were standing at the Public Welfare and you gave him one of those looks with your blue eyes. I wonder what he could say. Maybe: another fifteen went off yesterday. Funny how they get them to do it, when you think it's all voluntary and folk are paid no more for doing something than for doing nothing though they must need to eat more. Then I heard the one about Dr Ley and the cat and of course I saw the whole thing. You know that story?

THE SA MAN: No, we don't.

THE WORKER: Well, Dr Ley went on this little Strength Through Joy trip, strictly on business, and he met one of those former Weimar party bosses – I'm not up in all their names, anyway it might have been in a concentration camp though Dr Ley's got much too much sense to visit one of those – and the old boss asked him how'd he get the workers to swallow all the things they usedn't to put up with at any price. Dr Ley pointed to a cat lying in the sun and said: suppose you wanted to give that cat a mouthful of mustard and make her swallow it whether she wanted or not. How would you do it? Boss takes the mustard and smears it over the cat's chops; of course it spits it back in his face, no question of swallowing, just a lot of bloody scratches. No, old boy, says Dr Ley in his endearing way, you got the wrong approach. Now watch me. He takes the mustard with a practised follow-through and sticks it abracadabra up the wretched beast's arsehole. *To the ladies.* Excuse my French, but that's part of the story. – Numbed and stunned by the frightful pain, cat instantly sets to licking out the lot. There you are, my dear fellow, says the triumphant Dr Ley, she's eating it. And voluntarily at that!
They laugh.

THE WORKER: Yes, it's very funny.

THE SA MAN: That's got things going. Voluntary Labour Service, that's a favourite subject. Trouble is: nobody bothers to dig his toes in. Oh, they can make us eat shit and we'll still say thank you for it.

THE WORKER: I'm not so sure about that. There am I the other day on the Alexanderplatz wondering whether to volunteer for the Voluntary Labour Service spontaneous-like or wait till they shove me in. Over from the grocer's on the corner comes a skinny little woman, must be some proletarian's wife. Half a mo, says I, what are the proletarians doing in the Third Reich when we've got national unity and even Baron Thyssen is in it? No, says she, not when they've gone and put up the price of marge. From fifty pfennigs to one mark. You trying to tell me that's national unity? Better mind out, ma, says I, what you're saying to me, I'm patriotic to the backbone. All bones and no meat, says she, and chaff in the bread. She was that worked up. I just stand there mumbling: best get butter then. It's better for you. Mustn't skimp on your food, cause that saps the people's strength and we can't afford that what with so many enemies encircling us even in the top civil service . . . we been warned. No, says she, we're all of us Nazis so long as we got breath in our bodies, what mayn't be long now in view of the war menace. Only the other day I got to offer my best sofa to the Winter Aid, says she, cause I hear Goering's having to sleep on the floor he's that worried about our raw materials, and in the office they say they'd rather have a piano – you know, for Strength Through Joy. And no proper flour to be had. I takes my sofa away from the Winter Aid People and goes to the second-hand dealer round the corner, I been meaning to buy half a pound of butter for some time. And at the dairy they tell me: no butter today, comrade, would you like some guns? I say, give me, says she. I say: come on what d'you want guns for, ma? On an empty stomach? No, says she, if I'm going to be hungry they should be shot, the whole lot of them starting with Hitler at the top . . . Come on, says I, come on, exclaims I appalled . . . With Hitler at the top we'll conquer France, says she. Now we're getting our petrol from wool. And the wool? says I. The wool, says she: these days that's made from petrol. Wool's another thing we need. Any time a bit of good stuff from the old days reaches the Winter Aid the lot that run the place grab it for themselves, says she. If Hitler only knew, says they, but he knows nothing the poor lamb, never went to secondary school they say. I was struck dumb by so much subversiveness. You just stay here, young lady, says I, I got to make a call at police headquarters. But when I come back with an officer what d'you think, she's cleared off. *Stops play-acting.* What d'you say to that, eh?

THE SA MAN *still acting:* Me? What do I say? Well, I might give a reproachful look. You went straight round to the police, I might say. Can't risk talking freely when you're around.

THE WORKER: I should think not. Not with me. You confide in me, you'll be done. I know my duty as a comrade: any time my own mother mutters something to me about the price of margarine or something I go straight to the local SA office. I'll denounce my own brother for grumbling about the voluntary labour service. As for my girl, when she tells me 'Heil Hitler' she's got pregnant at a work camp then I have them bring her in: we can't have abortions because if we made exceptions for our nearest and dearest the Third Reich would run out of manpower, and the Third Reich's what we love best. – Was that more like it? Did I act all right?

THE SA MAN: I guess that'll do. *Goes on acting.* You'll be okay, go and draw your benefit, we've all understood, eh brothers? But you can count on me, my friend, 'nuff said, mum's the word. *He slaps him on the shoulder. No longer acting:* Right, then in you go into the office and they'll pick you up bang off.

THE WORKER: What, without you leaving the line and following me in?

THE SA MAN: Yeh.

THE WORKER: And without you giving someone a wink, which might look fishy?

THE SA MAN: Without me winking.

THE WORKER: How's it done then?

THE SA MAN: Ha, you'd like to know that trick. Well, stand up, and show us your back. *He turns him round by the shoulders, so that everyone can see his back. Then to the maidservant:* Seen it?

THE MAIDSERVANT: Look, he's got a white cross on it.

THE COOK: Right between his shoulders.

THE CHAUFFEUR: So he has.

THE SA MAN: And how did he get it? *Shows the palm of his*

hand. See, just a little white chalk cross and there's its impression large as life.

The worker takes off his jacket and looks at the cross.

THE WORKER: Nice work.

THE SA MAN: Not bad, eh? I always have my chalk on me. Ah, you have to use your loaf, things don't always go according to the book. *With satisfaction:* Well, so it's off to Reinickendorf. *Corrects himself:* That's where my aunt lives, you know. You lot don't seem very enthusiastic. *To the maidservant:* What are you gawping like that for, Anna? Missed the whole point of the trick, I suppose?

THE MAIDSERVANT: Of course not. Think I'm silly or something?

THE SA MAN *as if the whole joke has gone sour, stretches his hand out to her:* Wipe it off.

She washes his hand with a rag.

THE COOK: You've got to use those sort of methods so long as they keep on trying to undermine everything our Führer has built up and what makes other people so envious of us.

THE CHAUFFEUR: What was that? Oh yes, quite so. *Looks at his watch.* Well, time to wash the car again. Heil Hitler! *Exit.*

THE SA MAN: What kind of a fellow's that?

THE MAIDSERVANT: Keeps himself to himself. Not a bit political.

THE WORKER: Well, Minna, I'd better be off. No hard feelings about the beer, eh? And let me say I'm surer than ever that no one's going to complain about the Third Reich and get away with it. That's set my mind at rest. Me, I don't ever come across that sort of subversive element. I'd gladly confront them if I did. Only I'm not quite so quick to the punch as you. *Clearly and distinctly:* All right, Minna, thanks a lot and Heil Hitler!

THE OTHERS: Heil Hitler!

THE SA MAN: Take a tip from me and don't be quite so innocent. It attracts attention. No call to have to watch your mouth with me, I can take a joke now and again. All right: Heil Hitler!

The worker goes.

THE SA MAN: Bit sudden the way those two cleared out. Something's put ants in their pants. I shouldn't have said that about Reinickendorf. They're waiting to pounce on that sort of thing.

THE MAIDSERVANT: There's something else I wanted to ask you, Theo.

THE SA MAN: Fire away, any time.

THE COOK: I'm off to put out the laundry. I was young once too. *Exit.*

THE SA MAN: What is it?

THE MAIDSERVANT: But I shan't ask unless I can see you won't mind; otherwise I'll say nothing.

THE SA MAN: Spit it out, then.

THE MAIDSERVANT: It's just that . . . I don't like saying . . . well, I need 20 marks from our account.

THE SA MAN: Twenty marks?

THE MAIDSERVANT: There you are, you *do* mind.

THE SA MAN: Twenty marks out of our savings account, can't expect me to give three cheers. What do you want it for?

THE MAIDSERVANT: I'd rather not say.

THE SA MAN: So. You're not saying. That's a laugh.

THE MAIDSERVANT: I know you won't agree with me, Theo, so I'd sooner not give my reasons yet awhile.

THE SA MAN: Well, if you don't trust me . . .

THE MAIDSERVANT: Of course I trust you.

THE SA MAN: So you want to give up having a joint savings account?

THE MAIDSERVANT: How can you say that? If I take out twenty marks I'll still have ninety-seven marks left.

THE SA MAN: No need to do sums for my benefit. I know how much there is. I just think you're wanting to break it off, probably because you're flirting with someone else. Perhaps you'll be wanting to check our statement too.

THE MAIDSERVANT: I'm not flirting with anyone else.

THE SA MAN: Then tell me what it's for.

THE MAIDSERVANT: You don't want to let me have it.

THE SA MAN: How am I to tell it isn't for something wrong?

THE MAIDSERVANT: It's not anything wrong, and if I didn't need it I wouldn't call for it, you must know that.

THE SA MAN: I don't know nothing. All I know is the whole business strikes me as rather fishy. Why should you suddenly need twenty marks? It's quite a bit of money. You pregnant?

THE MAIDSERVANT: No.

THE SA MAN: Sure?

THE MAIDSERVANT: Yes.

THE SA MAN: If I thought for a minute you were planning anything illegal, if I caught a whiff of that kind of thing, I'd be down like a ton of bricks, let me tell you. You might just have heard that any interference with our burgeoning fruit is the worst crime you can commit. If the German people stopped multiplying itself it would be all up with our historic mission.

THE MAIDSERVANT: But Theo, I don't know what you're talking about. It's nothing like that, I'd have told you if it was because you'd be involved too. But if that's what you're thinking then let me tell you. It's just I want to help Frieda buy a winter coat.

THE SA MAN: And why can't your sister buy her coats for herself?

THE MAIDSERVANT: How could she on her disability pension, it's twenty-six marks eighty a month.

THE SA MAN: What about our Winter Aid? But that's just it, you've no confidence in our National Socialist state. I can tell that anyway from the sort of conversations that go on in this kitchen. Do you think I didn't see what a long face you pulled at my experiment?

THE MAIDSERVANT: What do you mean by a long face?

THE SA MAN: You pulled one all right. Just like our friends who cleared out so suddenly.

THE MAIDSERVANT: If you really want to know what I think, I don't like that kind of thing.

THE SA MAN: And what is it you don't like, may I ask?

THE MAIDSERVANT: The way you catch those poor down and outs by dressing up and playing tricks and all that. My father's unemployed too.

THE SA MAN: Ha, that's all I needed to hear. As if talking to that fellow Lincke hadn't already set me thinking.

THE MAIDSERVANT: Do you mean to say you're going to nail him for what he did just to please you and with all of us egging him on?

THE SA MAN: I'm not saying nothing. As I already told you. And if you've anything against what I'm doing as part of my duty then let me say just look in *Mein Kampf* and you'll see how the Führer himself didn't think it beneath him to test the people's attitude of mind, and it was actually his job for a while when he was in the army and it was all for Germany and the consequences were tremendously important.

THE MAIDSERVANT: If that's your line, Theo, then I'd just like to know if I can have the twenty marks. That's all.

THE SA MAN: Then all I can say to you is I'm not in the mood to have anything taken off me.

THE MAIDSERVANT: What do you mean, taken off you? Whose money is it, yours or mine?

THE SA MAN: That's a nice way to be speaking about our joint money all of a sudden. I suppose that's why we purged the Jews from the life of our nation, so we could have our own kith and kin suck our blood instead?

THE MAIDSERVANT: How can you say things like that on account of twenty marks?

THE SA MAN: I've plenty of expenses. My boots alone set me back twenty-seven marks.

THE MAIDSERVANT: But weren't they issued to you?

THE SA MAN: That's what we thought. And that's why I took the better kind, the ones with gaiters. Then they demanded payment and we were stung.

THE MAIDSERVANT: Twenty-seven marks for boots? So what other expenses were there?

THE SA MAN: What d'you mean, other expenses?

THE MAIDSERVANT: Didn't you say you had lots of expenses?

THE SA MAN: Forgotten what they were. Anyway I'm not here to be cross-examined. Keep your hair on, I'm not going to swindle you. And as for the twenty marks I'll think it over.

THE MAIDSERVANT *weeping:* Theo, I just can't believe you'd tell me the money was all right and it wasn't true. Oh now I don't know what to think. Surely there's twenty marks left in the savings bank out of all that money?

THE SA MAN *slapping her on the shoulder:* But nobody's suggesting for a minute that there's nothing left in our savings bank. Out of the question. You know you can rely on me. You trust something to me, it's like locking it in the safe. Well, decided to trust Theo again, have you?

She weeps without replying.

THE SA MAN: It's just nerves, you've been working too hard. Well, time I went off to that night exercise. I'll be coming for you on Friday, then. Heil Hitler! *Exit.*

The maidservant tries to suppress her tears and walks distractedly up and down the kitchen. The cook comes back with a basket of linen.

THE COOK: What's wrong? Had a quarrel? Theo's such a splendid boy. Pity there aren't more like him. Nothing serious, is it?

THE MAIDSERVANT *still weeping:* Minna, can't you go out to your brother's and tell him to watch out for himself?

THE COOK: What for?

THE MAIDSERVANT: Just watch out, I mean.

THE COOK: On account of tonight? You can't be serious. Theo would never do such a thing.

THE MAIDSERVANT: I don't know what to think any longer, Minna. He's changed so. They've completely ruined him. He's keeping bad company. Four years we've been going out together, and now it seems to me just as though . . . I even feel like asking you to look at my shoulder and see if there's a white cross on it.

4

Peat-bog soldiers

With storm troopers parading
These men carry on debating
What Lenin and Kautsky meant
Till, clutching the tomes they've cited
They're forcibly united
By joint imprisonment.

Esterwegen concentration camp, 1934. Some prisoners are mixing cement.

BRÜHL *softly to Dievenbach:* I'd steer clear of Lohmann; he talks.

DIEVENBACH *aloud:* Oi, Lohmann, here's Brühl saying I should steer clear of you; you talk.

BRÜHL: Bastard.

LOHMANN: That's good coming from you, you bloody Judas. Why did Karl get given solitary?

BRÜHL: Nothing to do with me. Was it me got cigarettes from God knows where?

THE JEHOVAH'S WITNESS: Look out.

The SS sentry up on the embankment goes by

THE SS MAN: Someone was talking here. Who was it? *Nobody answers.* If that happens just once more it'll be solitary confinement for the lot of you, get me? Now sing! *The prisoners sing verse 1 of the 'Song of the Peat-bog Soldiers'. The SS man moves on.*

'See, whichever way one gazes
Naught but boggy heath lies there.
Not one bird his sweet voice raises
In those oak trees gaunt and bare.
  We are the peat-bog soldiers
  With shovels on our shoulders
  We march.'

THE JEHOVAH'S WITNESS: Why do you people carry on quarreling even now?

DIEVENBACH: Don't you worry, Jehovah, you wouldn't understand. *Indicating Brühl:* Yesterday his party voted for Hitler's foreign policy in the Reichstag. And he – *indicating Lohmann* – thinks Hitler's foreign policy means war.

BRÜHL: Not with us around.

LOHMANN: Last war we had you were around all right.

BRÜHL: Anyway the German armed forces are too weak.

LOHMANN: Still, your lot did at least bring Hitler a battle-cruiser as part of the wedding deal.

THE JEHOVAH'S WITNESS *to Dievenbach:* What were you? Communist or Social-democrat?

DIEVENBACH: I kept outside all that.

LOHMANN: But you're inside now all right, inside a camp I mean.

THE JEHOVAH'S WITNESS: Look out.

The SS man appears again. He watches them, Slowly Brühl starts singing the third verse of the 'Song of the Peat-bog soldiers'. The SS man moves on.

'Back and forth the guards keep pacing
Not a soul can get away.
Shots for those who try escaping
Thick barbed wire for those who stay.
        We are the peat-bog soldiers
        With shovels on our shoulders
        We march.'

LOHMANN *hurls his shovel from him:* When I think I'm only in here because your lot sabotaged the united front I could bash your bloody brains out right now.

BRÜHL: Ha! 'Like your brother must I be/Or you'll turn and clobber me' – is that it? United front indeed. Softly softly catchee monkey: would have suited you nicely to sneak all our members away, wouldn't it?

LOHMANN: When you'd rather have Hitler sneak them away, like now. You traitors!

BRÜHL *furiously takes his shovel and brandishes it at Lohmann,*

who holds his own shovel at the ready: I'll teach you
something you won't forget!

THE JEHOVAH'S WITNESS: Look out.

*He hastily starts singing the last verse of the 'Song of the Peat-
bog soldiers'.*

*The SS man reappears and the others join in as they resume
mixing their cement.*

'We've no use for caterwauling.
Sunshine follows after rain.
One day soon you'll hear us calling:
Homeland, you are ours again.
  And then we peat-bog soldiers
  Will rise, throw back our shoulders
  And march.'

THE SS MAN: Which of you shouted 'Traitors'?

Nobody answers.

THE SS MAN: You people never learn, do you? *To Lohmann:*
Which?

Bohmann stares at Brühl and says nothing.

THE SS MAN *to Dievenbach:* Which?

Dievenbach says nothing.

THE SS MAN *to the Jehovah's Witness:* Which?

The Jehovah's Witness says nothing.

THE SS MAN *to Brühl:* Which?

Brühl says nothing.

THE SS MAN: I shall count up to five, then it'll be solitary
confinement for the whole lot of you till you turn blue.

*He waits for five seconds. They all stand in silence staring straight
ahead.*

THE SS MAN: So it's solitary.

5

Servants of the people

> The camps are run by warders
> Narks, butchers and marauders –
> The people's servants they
> They'll crush you and assail you
> And flog you and impale you
> For negligible pay.

Oranienburg Concentration Camp 1934. A small yard between the huts. In the darkness a sound of flogging. As it gets light an SS man is seen flogging a detainee. An SS officer stands in the background smoking; with his back to the scene. Then he goes off.

THE SS MAN *sits down on a barrel, exhausted:* Work on.

The detainee rises from the ground and starts unsteadily cleaning the drains.

Why can't you say no when they ask if you're a communist, you cunt? It means the lash for you and I have to stay in barracks. I'm so fucking tired. Why can't they give the job to Klapproth? He enjoys this sort of thing. Look, if that bastard comes round again – *he listens* – you're to take the whip and flog the ground hard as you can, right?

THE DETAINEE: Yes, sir.

THE SS MAN: But only because you buggers have flogged me out, right?

THE DETAINEE: Yes, sir.

THE SS MAN: Here he comes.

Steps are heard outside, and the SS man points to the whip. The detainee picks it up and flogs the ground. This doesn't sound authentic, so the SS man idly points to a nearby basket which the detainee then flogs. The steps outside come to a stop. The SS man abruptly rises in some agitation, snatches the whip and begins beating the detainee.

THE DETAINEE *softly:* Not my stomach.
The SS man hits him on the bottom. The SS officer looks in.
THE SS OFFICER: Flog his stomach.
The SS man beats the detainee's stomach.

6

Judicial process

The judges follow limply.
They were told that justice is simply
What serves our People best.
They objected: how are we to know that?
But they'll soon be interpreting it so that
The whole people is under arrest.

Augsburg 1934. Consultation room in a court building. A milky January morning can be seen through the window. A spherical gas lamp is still burning. The district judge is just putting on his robes. There is a knock.

THE JUDGE: Come in.
Enter the police inspector.
THE INSPECTOR: Good morning, your honour.
THE JUDGE: Good morning, Mr Tallinger. It's about the case of Häberle, Schünt and Gaunitzer. I must admit the whole affair is a bit beyond me.
THE INSPECTOR:?
THE JUDGE: I understand from the file that the shop where the incident occurred – Arndt's the jeweller's – is a Jewish one?
THE INSPECTOR:?
THE JUDGE: And presumably Häberle, Schünt and Gaunitzer are still members of Storm Troop 7?
The inspector nods.

THE JUDGE: Which means that the Troop saw no reason to discipline them?

The inspector shakes his head.

THE JUDGE: All the same, I take it the Troop must have instituted some kind of inquiry in view of the disturbance which the incident caused in the neighbourhood?

The inspector shrugs his shoulders.

THE JUDGE: I would appreciate it, Tallinger, if you would give me a brief summary before we go into court. Would you?

THE INSPECTOR *mechanically:* On 2 December 1933 at 0815 hours SA men Häberle, Schünt and Gaunitzer forced their way into Arndt's jewellers in the Schlettowstrasse and after a brief exchange of words wounded Mr Arndt age 54 on the head. The material damage amounted to a total of eleven thousand two hundred and thirty-four marks. Inquiries were instituted by the criminal investigation department on 7 December 1933 and led to . . .

THE JUDGE: Come on, Tallinger, that's all in the files. *He points irritably at the charge sheet, which consists of a single page.* This is the flimsiest and sloppiest made-out indictment I've ever seen, not that the last few months have been much of a picnic, let me tell you. But it does say that much. I was hoping you might be able to tell me a bit about the background.

THE INSPECTOR: Yes, your honour.

THE JUDGE: Well, then?

THE INSPECTOR: There isn't any background to this case, your honour, so to speak.

THE JUDGE: Tallinger, are you trying to tell me it's all clear as daylight?

THE INSPECTOR *grinning:* Clear as daylight: no.

THE JUDGE: Various items of jewellery are alleged to have vanished in the course of the incident. Have they been recovered?

THE INSPECTOR: Not to my knowledge: no.

THE JUDGE: ?

THE INSPECTOR: Your honour, I've got a family.

THE JUDGE: So have I, Tallinger.

top you dragging it up. Any of the local witnesses might
mention it.

THE JUDGE: I see. But I can't see much else.

THE INSPECTOR: The less the better, if you want my personal opinion.

THE JUDGE: It's easy for you to say that. I have to deliver
a judgement.

THE INSPECTOR *vaguely:* That's right . . .

THE JUDGE: So we're left with a direct provocation on
Arndt's part, or else there's no way of explaining what
happened.

THE INSPECTOR: Just what I'd say myself, your honour.

THE JUDGE: Then how were those SA people provoked?

THE INSPECTOR: According to their statements: partly by
Arndt himself and partly by some unemployed man he'd got
in to sweep the snow. Apparently they were on their way to
have a beer together and as they passed the shop there were
Wagner the unemployed man and Arndt himself standing in
the doorway and shouting vulgar terms of abuse at them.

THE JUDGE: I don't suppose they have any witnesses, have
they?

THE INSPECTOR: Oh, they have. The landlord – you know,
von Miehl – said he was at the window and saw Wagner
provoking the SA men. And Arndt's partner, a man called
Stau, was round at Troop HQ the same afternoon and
admitted in front of Häberle, Schünt and Gaunitzer that
Arndt had always talked disparagingly about the SA, to
him too.

THE JUDGE: Oh, so Arndt's got a partner? Aryan?

THE INSPECTOR: Aryan: what else? Can you really see him
taking on a Jew as his front man?

THE JUDGE: But the partner wouldn't go and give evidence
against him?

THE INSPECTOR *slyly:* Who's to say?

THE JUDGE *irritated:* What do you mean? There's no way
the firm can claim damages if it can be proved that Arndt
provoked Häberle, Schünt and Gaunitzer to assault him.

THE INSPECTOR: What makes you think Stau's interested
in claiming damages?

THE INSPECTOR: Yes, sir.

Pause.

THE INSPECTOR: This Arndt fellow is a Jew, yo

THE JUDGE: So one would infer from the name.

THE INSPECTOR: Yes, sir, There's been a rumour
time in the neighbourhood that there was a case
profanation.

THE JUDGE *begins to get a glimmer:* Indeed. Inv
whom?

THE INSPECTOR: Arndt's daughter. She's ninetee
supposed to be pretty.

THE JUDGE: Was there any official follow-up?

THE INSPECTOR *reluctantly:* Well, no. The rumour di
natural death.

THE JUDGE: Who set it going?

THE INSPECTOR: The landlord of the building. A certa
Mr von Miehl.

THE JUDGE: I suppose he wanted the Jewish shop out o
his building?

THE INSPECTOR: That's what we thought. But then he
seems to have changed his line.

THE JUDGE: At least that would explain why there w
certain amount of resentment against Arndt round th
Leading these young people to act from a kind of ups
of national feeling . . .

THE INSPECTOR *firmly:* I wouldn't say that, your hor

THE JUDGE: What wouldn't you say?

THE INSPECTOR: That Häberle, Schünt and Gaunitze
try to get much mileage out of the racial profanation
ness.

THE JUDGE: Why not?

THE INSPECTOR: As I told you, there hasn't bee
official mention of the name of the Aryan invol
could be anyone. Anywhere there's a bunch of
you might find him, you get me? And where d'y
those bunches of Aryans? In other words the SA
want this dragged up.

THE JUDGE *impatiently:* Why tell me about it, then?

THE INSPECTOR: Because you said you'd got a fan

THE JUDGE: I don't get you. Surely he's a partner?

THE INSPECTOR: That's it.

THE JUDGE: ?

THE INSPECTOR: We've found out – unofficially of course and off the record – that Stau's a regular visitor to Troop HQ. He used to be in the SA and may still be. Probably that's what made Arndt make him a partner. What's more, Stau's already been mixed up in a similar affair, where the SA dropped in on someone. They picked the wrong man that time and it took quite a bit of effort to get it all swept under the mat. Of course that's not to say that in our particular case Stau ... Well, anyhow he's someone to be careful of. I hope you'll treat this as completely confidential, given what you said about your family earlier.

THE JUDGE *shaking his head:* I don't quite see how it can be in Mr Stau's interest for his business to lose more than eleven thousand marks.

THE INSPECTOR: Yes, the jewellery has disappeared. Anyhow Häberle, Schünt and Gaunitzer haven't got it. And they haven't fenced it either.

THE JUDGE: Indeed.

THE INSPECTOR: Stau naturally can't be expected to keep Arndt on as his partner if Arndt can be shown to have acted in a provocative way. And any loss he has caused will have to made up to Stau, see?

THE JUDGE: Yes, I do indeed see. *For a moment he looks thoughtfully at the inspector, who resumes his blank official expression.* Yes, then I suppose the long and the short of it will be that Arndt provoked the SA men. It seems that the fellow had made himself generally disliked. Didn't you tell me that the goings-on in his own family had already led the landlord to complain? Ah well, I know this shouldn't really be dragged up, but anyway we can take it that there will be relief in those quarters if he moves out shortly. Thank you very much, Tallinger, you've been a great help.

The judge gives the inspector a cigar. The inspector leaves. In the doorway he meets the official prosecutor, who is just entering.

THE PROSECUTOR *to the judge:* Can I have a word with you?

THE JUDGE *as he peels an apple for his breakfast:* You can indeed.

THE PROSECUTOR: It's about the case of Häberle, Schünt and Gaunitzer.

THE JUDGE *otherwise occupied:* Yes?

THE PROSECUTOR: It seems quite a straightforward case on the face of it . . .

THE JUDGE: Right. I really don't see why your department decided to prosecute, if you don't mind my saying so.

THE PROSECUTOR: What do you mean? The case has caused a deplorable stir in the neighbourhood. Even members of the party have thought it ought to be cleared up.

THE JUDGE: I simply see it as a plain case of Jewish provocation, that's all.

THE PROSECUTOR: Oh, rubbish, Goll! Don't imagine our indictments can be dismissed so lightly just because they seem a bit tersely expressed these days. I could have guessed you'd blithely settle for the most obvious interpretation. Better not make a boob of this. It doesn't take long to get transferred to the Silesian backwoods. And it's not all that cosy there these days.

THE JUDGE *puzzled, stops eating his apple:* I don't understand that one little bit. Are you seriously telling me you propose to let the Jew Arndt go free?

THE PROSECUTOR *expansively:* You bet I am. The fellow had no idea of provoking anyone. Are you suggesting that because he's Jewish he can't expect justice in the courts of the Third Reich? That's some pretty queer opinions you're venting there, Goll.

THE JUDGE *irritably:* I was venting no opinions whatever. I simply concluded that Häberle, Schünt and Gaunitzer were provoked.

THE PROSECUTOR: But can't you see it wasn't Arndt who provoked them but that unemployed fellow, what's his damn name, the one clearing the snow, yes, Wagner?

THE JUDGE: There's not one single word about that in your indictment, my dear Spitz.

THE PROSECUTOR: Of course not. It merely came to the attention of the Prosecutor's office that those SA men had made an assault on Arndt. Which meant that we were officially bound to take action. But if witness von Miehl should testify in court that Arndt wasn't in the street at all during the dispute, whereas that unemployed fellow, what's his damn name, yes, Wagner, was hurling insults at the SA, then it will have to be taken into account.

THE JUDGE *tumbling to earth:* Is that what von Miehl is supposed to be saying? But he's the landlord who wants to get Arndt out of his building. He's not going to give evidence for him.

THE PROSECUTOR: Come on, what have you got against von Miehl? Why shouldn't he tell the truth under oath? Perhaps you don't realise that, quite apart from the fact that he's in the SS, von Miehl has pretty good contacts in the Ministry of Justice? My advice to you, Goll old man, is to treat him as a man of honour.

THE JUDGE: That's what I'm doing. After all, you can't call it exactly a dishonourable these days not to want a Jewish shop in one's building.

THE PROSECUTOR *generously:* If the fellow pays his rent . . .

THE JUDGE *diplomatically:* I believe he's supposed to have reported him already on another matter . . .

THE PROSECUTOR: So you're aware of that? But who told you it was in order to get the fellow out? Particularly as the complaint was withdrawn? That suggests something more like a particularly close understanding, wouldn't you say? My dear Goll, how can you be so naif?

THE JUDGE *now getting really annoyed:* My dear Spitz, it's not that simple. The partner I thought would want to cover him wants to report him, and the landlord who reported him wants to cover him. You have to know the ins and outs.

THE PROSECUTOR: What do we draw our pay for?

THE JUDGE: Shockingly mixed-up business. Have a Havana?

The prosecutor takes a Havana and they smoke in silence. Then the judge gloomily reflects.

THE JUDGE: But suppose it's established in court that Arndt never provoked anybody, then he can go on and sue the SA for damages.

THE PROSECUTOR: To start with he can't sue the SA but only Häberle, Schünt and Gaunitzer, who haven't a penny – that's if he doesn't simply have to make do with that unemployed fellow, what's his damn name ... got it, Wagner. *With emphasis:* Secondly he may think twice before suing members of the SA.

THE JUDGE: Where is he at the moment?

THE PROSECUTOR: In hospital.

THE JUDGE: And Wagner?

THE PROSECUTOR: In a concentration camp.

THE JUDGE *with a certain relief:* Oh well, in those circumstances I don't suppose Arndt will be wanting to sue the SA. And Wagner won't be particularly keen to make a big thing of his innocence. But the SA aren't going to be all that pleased if the Jew gets off scot free.

THE PROSECUTOR: The SA will have proof in court that they were provoked. By the Jew or by the Marxist, it's all the same to them.

THE JUDGE *still dubious:* Not entirely. After all the dispute between the SA and the unemployed man did result in damage to the shop. Storm Troop 7 isn't altogether in the clear.

THE PROSECUTOR: Oh well, you can't have everything. You'll never be able to satisfy all parties. As for which you should aim to satisfy, that's a matter for your sense of patriotism, my dear Goll. All I can say is that patriotic circles – by which I mean the highest quarters of the SS – are looking to the German judiciary to show a bit more backbone.

THE JUDGE *with a deep sigh:* The process of law is getting a bit complicated these days, my dear Spitz, you must admit.

THE PROSECUTOR: Of course. But you have an excellent remark by our Minister of Justice to guide you. Justice is what serves the German people best.

THE JUDGE *apathetically:* Mm yes.

THE PROSECUTOR: Mustn't let it get you down, that's all. *He gets up.* So now you've got the background. Should be plain sailing. See you later, my dear Goll.

He leaves. The judge is not at all happy. He stands by the window for a while. Then he leafs aimlessly through his papers. Finally he presses the bell. A court usher enters.

THE JUDGE: Go and find Detective-Inspector Tallinger in the witnesses' room and bring him back here. Discreetly. *Exit the usher. Then the inspector reappears.*

THE JUDGE: Tallinger, you nearly landed me in the cart with your idea of treating this as a case of provocation on Arndt's part. Apparently Mr von Miehl is all set to swear that it was Wagner the unemployed man who did the provoking and not Arndt.

THE INSPECTOR *giving nothing away:* So they say, your honour.

THE JUDGE: What's that mean: 'so they say'?

THE INSPECTOR: That Wagner shouted the offensive remarks.

THE JUDGE: Isn't it true?

THE INSPECTOR *offended:* Your honour, whether it's true or not it's not something we can . . .

THE JUDGE *firmly:* Listen to me, Detective-Inspector Tallinger. This is a German court you're in. Has Wagner admitted that or has he not?

THE INSPECTOR: Your honour, I didn't go to the concentration camp myself, if you want to know. The official report of his deposition – Wagner's supposed to have got something wrong with his kidneys – says that he admitted it. It's only that . . .

THE JUDGE: There you are, he did admit it. It's only that what?

THE INSPECTOR: He served in the war and was wounded in the neck, and according to Stau, you know, Arndt's partner, he can't talk above a whisper. So how von Miehl could have heard him from the first floor hurling insults isn't entirely . . .

THE JUDGE: I imagine it will be said that you don't need a voice in order to tell someone to 'get stuffed', as they put it. You can do it with a simple gesture. It's my impression the Prosecutor's department want to provide the SA with some way out of that sort. More precisely, of that sort and no other.

THE INSPECTOR: Yes, your honour.

THE JUDGE: What is Arndt's statement?

THE INSPECTOR: That he had no part in it and just hurt his head falling down the stairs. That's all we can get out of him.

THE JUDGE: The fellow's probably quite innocent and got into it accidentally, like Pontius Pilate and the Creed.

THE INSPECTOR *gives up:* Yes, your honour.

THE JUDGE: And it should be good enough for the SA if their men get off.

THE INSPECTOR: Yes, your honour.

THE JUDGE: Don't stand there saying 'yes, your honour' like a damn metronome.

THE INSPECTOR: Yes, your honour.

THE JUDGE: What are you trying to tell me? Don't get on your high horse now, Tallinger. You must make allowances for my being a bit on edge. I realise you're an honest man. And when you advised me you must have had something at the back of your mind?

THE INSPECTOR *being a kindly soul, plunges in:* Hasn't it struck you that our deputy prosecutor might simply be after your job and is putting the skids under you, sir? That's what they're saying. – Look at it this way, your honour: you find the Jew not guilty. He never provoked a soul. Wasn't around. Got his head bashed in by pure accident, some quarrel between a different lot of people. Then after a while, back he comes to the shop. No way Stau can prevent it. And the shop is about eleven thousand marks short. Stau will be just as hit by this loss, because now he can't claim the eleven thousand back from Arndt. So Stau, from what I know of his sort, is going to tackle the SA about his jewels. He can't approach them in person because being in partnership with a Jew counts as being sold out to Judah. But he'll have people who can. Then it will come out that the SA go pinching jewels in an upsurge of national feeling. You can guess for yourself how Storm Troop 7 is going to look at your verdict. And the man in the street won't understand anyway. Because how can it be possible for a Jew to win a case against the SA under the Third Reich?

For some while there has been noise off. It now becomes quite loud.

THE JUDGE: What's that shocking noise? Just a minute, Tallinger. *He rings. The usher comes in.* What's that din, man?

THE USHER: The courtroom's full. And now they're jammed so tight in the corridors that nobody can get through. And there are some people from the SA there who say they've got to get through because they've orders to attend.

Exit the usher, while the judge just looks scared.

THE INSPECTOR *continuing:* Those people are going to be a bit of a nuisance to you, you know. I'd advise you to concentrate on Arndt and not stir up the SA.

THE JUDGE *sits brokenly, holding his head in his hands. In a weary voice:* All right, Tallinger, I'll have to think it over.

THE INSPECTOR: That's the idea, your honour.

He leaves. The judge gets up with difficulty and rings insistently. Enter the usher.

THE JUDGE: Just go over and ask Judge Fey of the High Court if he'd mind looking in for a moment.

The usher goes. Enter the judge's maidservant with his packed breakfast.

THE MAIDSERVANT: You'll be forgetting your own head next, your honour. You're a terrible man. What did you forget this time? Try and think. The most important thing of all! *She hands him the packet.* Your breakfast! You'll be going off again and buying those rolls hot from the oven and next thing we'll have another stomach-ache like last week. Because you don't look after yourself properly.

THE JUDGE: That'll do, Marie.

THE MAIDSERVANT: Had a job getting through, I did. The whole building's full of brownshirts on account of the trial. But they'll get it hot and strong today, won't they, your honour? Like at the butcher's folk were saying 'good thing there's still some justice left'. Going and beating a business man up! Half the SA used to be criminals; it's common knowledge in the neighbourhood. If we didn't have justice they'd be making away with the cathedral. After the rings, they were; that Häberle's got a girl friend who was on the game till six months ago. And they attacked Wagner, him with the neck wound and no job, when he was shovelling snow with everyone looking on. They're quite open about it, just terrorising the neighbourhood, and if anybody says anything they lay for him and beat him senseless.

THE JUDGE: All right, Marie. Just run along now.

THE MAIDSERVANT: I told them in the butcher's: his honour will show them where they get off, right? All the decent folk are on your side, that's a fact, your honour. Only don't eat your breakfast too quickly, it might do you harm. It's so bad for the health, and now I'll be off and not hold you up, you'll have to be going into court, and don't get worked up in court or perhaps you'd better eat first, it'll only take a few minutes and they won't matter and you shouldn't eat when your stomach's all tensed up. Because you should take better care of yourself. Your health's your most precious possession, but now I'll be off, there's no need to tell you and I can see you're raring to get on with the case and I've got to go to the grocer's still.

Exit the maidservant. Enter Judge Fey of the High Court, an elderly judge with whom the district judge is friends.

THE SENIOR JUDGE: What's up?

THE JUDGE: I've got something I'd like to discuss with you if you've a moment. I'm sitting on a pretty ghastly case this morning.

THE SENIOR JUDGE: *sitting down:* I know, the SA case.

THE JUDGE *stops pacing around:* How d'you know about that?

THE SENIOR JUDGE: It came up in discussion yesterday afternoon. A nasty business.

The judge starts again nervously pacing up and down.

THE JUDGE: What are they saying over your side?

THE SENIOR JUDGE: You aren't envied. *Intrigued:* What'll you do?

THE JUDGE: That's just what I'd like to know. I must say I didn't realise this case had become so famous.

THE SENIOR JUDGE: *slightly amazed:* Indeed?

THE JUDGE: That partner is said to be a rather disagreeable customer.

THE SENIOR JUDGE: So I gather. Not that von Miehl is much of a humanitarian either.

THE JUDGE: Is anything known about him?

THE SENIOR JUDGE: Enough to go on with. He's got those sort of contacts.

Pause.

THE JUDGE: Very high ones?

THE SENIOR JUDGE: Very high.

Pause.

THE SENIOR JUDGE: *cautiously:* Suppose you leave the Jew out of it and acquit Häberle, Schünt and Gaunitzer on the ground that the unemployed man provoked them before he dodged back into the shop, I imagine the SA might find that all right? Arndt won't sue the SA in any case.

THE JUDGE *anxiously:* There's Arndt's partner. He'll go to the SA and ask for his valuables back. And then, you know, Fey, I'll have the whole SA leadership gunning for me.

THE SENIOR JUDGE *after considering this argument, which apparently has taken him by surprise:* But suppose you don't leave the Jew out of it, then von Miehl will bring bigger guns to bear, to put it mildly. Perhaps you didn't realise he's being pressed by his bank? Arndt's his lifebelt.

THE JUDGE *appalled:* Pressed by his bank!

There is a knock.

THE SENIOR JUDGE: Come in!

Enter the usher.

THE USHER: Your honour, I really don't know what to do about keeping seats for the Chief State Prosecutor and President Schönling of the High Court. If only their honours would let one know in time.

THE SENIOR JUDGE *since the judge says nothing:* Clear two seats and don't interrupt us.

Exit the usher.

THE JUDGE: That's something I could have done without.

THE SENIOR JUDGE: Whatever happens, von Miehl can't afford to abandon Arndt and let him be ruined. He needs him.

THE JUDGE *crushed:* Someone he can milk.

THE SENIOR JUDGE: I said nothing of the sort, my dear Goll. And it seems to me quite extraordinary that you should imply I did. Let me make it crystal clear that I've not said one word against Mr von Miehl. I regret having to do so, Goll.

THE JUDGE *getting worked up:* But Fey, you can't take it that way. Not in view of our mutual relationship.

THE SENIOR JUDGE: What on earth do you mean, 'our mutual relationship'? I can't interfere in your cases. You have to choose for yourself whose toes you are going to tread on, the SA or the Ministry of Justice; either way it's your decision and nobody else's. These days everybody's his own best friend.

THE JUDGE: Of course I'm my own best friend. But what do I advise myself to do?

He stands by the door, listening to the noise outside.

THE SENIOR JUDGE: A bad business.

THE JUDGE *agitatedly:* I'll do anything, my God, can't you see my position? You've changed so. I'll give my judgement this way or that way, whatever way they want me to, but I've got to know first what they want me to do. If one doesn't know that, there's no justice left.

THE SENIOR JUDGE: I wouldn't go round shouting that there's no justice left if I were you, Goll.

THE JUDGE: Oh God, what have I said now? That's not what I meant. I just mean that with so many conflicting interests . . .

THE SENIOR JUDGE: There are no conflicting interests in the Third Reich.

THE JUDGE: Of course not. I wasn't saying there were. Don't keep weighing every single word of mine on your scales.

THE SENIOR JUDGE: Why shouldn't I? I am a judge.

THE JUDGE *who is breaking into a sweat:* But Fey, if every word uttered by every judge had to be weighed like that! I'm prepared to go over everything in the most careful and conscientious possible way, but I have to be told what kind of a decision will satisfy higher considerations. If I allow the

Jew to have stayed inside the shop then I'll upset the landlord – I mean the partner; I'm getting muddled – and if the
provocation came from the unemployed man then it'll be
the landlord who – yes, but von Miehl would rather – Look,
they can't pack me off to the backwoods in Silesia, I've got
a hernia and I'm not getting embroiled with the SA, Fey,
after all I've a family. It's easy for my wife to say I should
just find out what actually happened. I'd wake up in hospital
if nothing worse. Do I talk about assault? No, I'll talk
about provocation. So what's wanted? I shan't condemn the
SA of course but only the Jew or the unemployed man,
only which of the two should I condemn? How do I decide
between unemployed man and Jew or between partner and
landlord. Whatever happens I'm not going to Silesia, Fey,
I'd rather a concentration camp, the whole thing's impossible. Don't look at me like that. I'm not in the dock.
I'm prepared to do absolutely anything.

THE SENIOR JUDGE *who has got to his feet:* Being prepared
isn't enough, my dear fellow.

THE JUDGE: But how am I to make my decision?

THE SENIOR JUDGE: Usually a judge goes by what his
conscience tells him, Judge Goll. Let that be your guide.
It has been a pleasure.

THE JUDGE: Yes, of course: to the best of my heart and
conscience. But here and now; what's my choice to be,
Fey? What?

*The senior judge has left. The judge looks wordlessly after him.
The telephone rings.*

THE JUDGE *picks up the receiver:* Yes? – Emmy? – What
have they put off? Our skittles session? – Who was it
rang? – Priesnitz, the one who's just taken his finals?
Where did he get the message? – What I'm talking about?
I've got a judgement to deliver.

*He hangs up. The usher enters. The noise in the corridors becomes
obtrusive.*

THE USHER: Häberle, Schünt, Gaunitzer, your honour.

THE JUDGE *collecting his papers:* One moment.

THE USHER: I've put the President of the High Court at
the press table. He was quite happy about it. But the Chief

State Prosecutor refused to take a seat among the witnesses. He wanted to be on the bench, I think. Then you'd have had to preside from the dock, your honour! *He laughs foolishly at his own joke.*

THE JUDGE: Whatever happens I'm not doing that.

THE USHER: This way out, your honour. But where's your folder got to with the indictment?

THE JUDGE *utterly confused:* Oh yes, I'll need that. Or I won't know who's being accused, will I? What the devil are we to do with the Chief State Prosecutor?

THE USHER: But your honour, that's your address book you've picked up. Here's the file.

He pushes it under the judge's arm. Wiping the sweat off his face, the judge goes distractedly out.

7

Occupational disease

And as for the physicians
The State gives them positions
And pays them so much a piece.
Their job is to keep mending
The bits the police keep sending
Then send it all back to the police.

Berlin 1934. A ward in the Charité Hospital. A new patient has been brought in. Nurses are busy writing his name on the slate at the head of his bed. Two patients in neighbouring beds are talking.

THE FIRST PATIENT: Know anything about him?

THE SECOND: I saw them bandaging him downstairs. He was on a stretcher quite close to me. He was still conscious then, but when I asked what he'd got he didn't answer. His whole body's one big wound.

THE FIRST: No need to ask then, was there?

THE SECOND: I didn't see till they started bandaging him.

ONE OF THE NURSES: Quiet please, it's the professor.

Followed by a train of assistants and nurses the surgeon enters the ward. He stops by one of the beds and pontificates.

THE SURGEON: Gentlemen, we have here a quite beautiful case showing how essential it is to ask questions and keep on searching for the deeper causes of the disease if medicine is not to degenerate into mere quackery. This patient has all the symptoms of neuralgia and for a considerable time he received the appropriate treatment. In fact however he suffers from Raynaud's Disease, which he contracted in the course of his job as a worker operating pneumatically powered tools; that is to say, gentlemen, an occupational disease. We have now begun treating him correctly. His case will show you what a mistake it is to treat the patient as a mere component of the clinic instead of asking where he has come from, how did he contract his disease and what he will be going back to once treatment is concluded. There are three things a good doctor has to be able to do. What are they? The first?

THE FIRST ASSISTANT: Ask questions.

THE SURGEON: The second?

THE SECOND ASSISTANT: Ask questions.

THE SURGEON: And the third?

THE THIRD ASSISTANT: Ask questions, sir.

THE SURGEON: Correct. Ask questions. Particularly concerning . . .?

THE THIRD ASSISTANT: The social conditions, sir.

THE SURGEON: The great thing is never to be shy of looking into the patient's private life – often a regrettably depressing one. If someone is forced to follow some occupation that is bound in the long run to destroy his body, so that he dies in effect to avoid starving to death, one doesn't much like hearing about it and consequently doesn't ask.

He and his followers move on to the new patient.

What has this man got?

The sister whispers in his ear.
Oh, I see.
He gives him a cursory examination with evident reluctance.
Dictates: Contusions on the back and thighs. Open wounds on the abdomen. Further symptoms?

THE SISTER *reads out:* Blood in his urine.

THE SURGEON: Diagnosis on admission?

THE SISTER: Lesion to left kidney.

THE SURGEON: Get him X-rayed. *Starts to turn away.*

THE THIRD ASSISTANT *who has been taking down his medical history:* How was that incurred, sir?

THE SURGEON: What have they put?

THE SISTER: Falling downstairs, it says here.

THE SURGEON *dictating:* A fall down the stairs. Why are his hands tied that way, Sister?

THE SISTER: The patient has twice torn his dressings off, professor.

THE SURGEON: Why?

THE FIRST PATIENT *sotto voce:* Where has the patient come from and where is he going back to?
All heads turn in his direction.

THE SURGEON *clearing his throat:* If this patient seems disturbed give him morphine. *Moves on to the next bed:* Feeling better now? It won't be long before you're fit as a fiddle. *He examines the patient's neck.*

ONE ASSISTANT *to another:* Worker. Brought in from Oranienburg.

THE OTHER ASSISTANT *grinning:* Another case of occupational disease, I suppose.

8

The physicists

Enter the local Newtons
Dressed up like bearded Teutons –
Not one of them hook-nosed.
Their science will end up barbarian
For they'll get an impeccably Aryan
State-certified physics imposed.

Göttingen 1935. Institute for Physics. Two scientists, X and Y. Y has just entered. He has a conspiratorial look.

Y: I've got it.

X: What?

Y: The answer to what we asked Mikovsky in Paris.

X: About gravity waves?

Y: Yes.

X: What about it?

Y: Guess who's written giving just what we wanted.

X: Go on.

Y takes a scrap of paper writes a name and passes it to X. As soon as X has read it Y takes it back, tears it into small pieces and throws it into the stove.

Y: Mikovsky passed our questions on to him. This is his answer.

X *grabs for it greedily:* Give me. *He suddenly holds himself back.* Just suppose we were caught corresponding with him like this . . .

Y: We absolutely mustn't be.

X: Well, without it we're stuck. Come on, give me.

Y: You won't be able to read. I used my own shorthand, it's safer. I'll read it out to you.

X: For God's sake be careful.

Y: Is Rollkopf in the lab today? *He points to the right.*

X: *pointing to the left:* No, but Reinhardt is. Sit over here.

y *reads:* The problem concerns two arbitrary countervariant vectors *psi* and *nu* and a countervariant vector *t.* This is used to form the elements of a mixed tensor of the second degree whose structure can be expressed by $\Sigma^{-lr} = C^{-l}_{bi}.$

x *who has been writing this down, suddenly gives him a sign to shut up:* Just a minute.

He gets up and tiptoes over to the wall, left. Having evidently heard nothing suspicious he returns. Y goes on reading aloud, with other similar interruptions. These lead them to inspect the telephone, suddenly open the door etc.

y: Where matter is passive, incoherent and not acting on itself by means of tensions $T = \mu$ will be the only component of the tensional energy depth that differs from o. Hence a static gravitational field is created whose equation, taking into account the constant proportionality factor $8\pi x$ will be $\Delta f = 4\pi x\mu$. Given a suitable choice of spatial coordinates the degree of variation from $c^2 dt^2$ will be very slight . . .

A door slams somewhere and they try to hide their notes. Then this seems to be unnecessary. From this point on they both become engrossed in the material and apparently oblivious of the danger of what they are doing.

y *reads on:* . . . by comparison however with the passive mass from which the field originates the masses concerned are very small, and the motion of the bodies implicated in the gravitational field is brought within this static field by means of a geodetic world line. As such this satisfies the variational principle $\delta\int ds = o$ where the ends of the relevant portion of the world line remain fixed.

x: But what's Einstein got to say about . . .

Y's look of horror makes X aware of his mistake so that he sits there paralysed with shock. Y snatches the notes which he has been taking down and hides away all the papers.

y *very loudly, in the direction of the left hand wall:* What a typical piece of misplaced Jewish ingenuity. Nothing to do with physics.

Relieved, they again bring out their notes and silently resume work, using the utmost caution.

9

The Jewish wife

Over there we can see men coming
Whom He's forced to relinquish their women
And coupled with blondes in their place.
It's no good their cursing and praying
For once He catches them racially straying
He'll whip them back into the Race.

Frankfurt 1935. It is evening. A woman is packing suitcases. She is choosing what to take. Now and again she removes something from her suitcase and returns it to its original place in the room in order to pack another item instead. For a long while she hesitates whether to take a large photograph of her husband that stands on the chest of drawers. Finally she leaves the picture where it is. The packing tires her and for a time she sits on a suitcase leaning her head on her hand. Then she gets to her feet and telephones.

THE WOMAN: This is Judith Keith. Hullo, is that you, doctor? Good evening. I just wanted to ring up and say you'll have to be looking for another bridge partner; I'm going away. – No, not long, but anyway a few weeks   I want to go to Amsterdam. – Yes, it's said to be lovely there in spring. – I've got friends there. – No, plural, believe it or not. – Who will you get for a fourth? – Come on, we haven't played for a fortnight. – That's right, Fritz had a cold too. It's absurd to go on playing bridge when it's as cold as this, I always say. – But no, doctor, how could I? – Anyway Thekla had her mother there. – I know. – What put that idea into my head? – No, it was nothing sudden, I kept putting it off, and now I've really got to . . . Right, we'll have to cancel our cinema date, remember me to Thekla. – Ring him up on a Sunday sometimes, could you perhaps? – Well, au revoir! – Yes, of course I will. – Goodbye.
She hangs up and calls another number.

This is Judith Keith. Can I speak to Frau Schöck? –
Lotte? – I just wanted to say goodbye. I'm going away
for a bit. – No, nothing's wrong, it's just that I want
to see some new faces. – I really meant to say that Fritz
has got the Professor coming here on Tuesday evening,
and I wondered if you could both come too, I'm off
tonight as I said. – Tuesday, that's it. – No, I only
wanted to tell you I'm off tonight, there's no connec-
tion, I just thought you might be able to come then. –
Well, let's say even though I shan't be there, right? –
Yes, I know you're not that sort, but what about it,
these are unsettled times and everybody's being so careful, so you'll come? – It depends on Max? He'll manage
it, the Professor will be there, tell him. – I must ring
off now. – Goodbye then.

She hangs up and calls another number.

That you, Gertrud? It's Judith. I'm so sorry to disturb
you. – Thanks, I just wanted to ask if you could see that
Fritz is all right, I'm going away for a few months. –
Being his sister, I thought you . . . Why not? – Nobody'd
think that, anyway not Fritz. – Well, of course he knows
we don't . . . get on all that well, but . . . Then he can
simply call you if you prefer it that way. – Yes, I'll tell
him that. – Everything's fairly straight, of course the flat's
on the big side. – You'd better leave his workroom to Ida
to deal with, she knows what's to be done. – I find her
pretty intelligent, and he's used to her. – And there's another thing, I hope you don't mind my saying so, but he
doesn't like talking before meals, can you remember that?
I always used to watch myself. – I don't want to argue
about that just now, it's not long till my train goes and I
haven't finished packing, you know. – Keep an eye on his
suits and remind him to go to his tailor, he's ordered a
new overcoat, and do see that his bedroom's properly
heated, he likes sleeping with the window open and it's
too cold. – No, I don't think he needs to toughen himself
up, but I must ring off now. – I'm very grateful to you,
Gertrud, and we'll write to each other, won't we? –
Goodbye.

She hangs up and calls another number.

Anna? It's Judith; look, I'm just off. – No, there's no way out, things are getting too difficult. – Too difficult! – Well, no, it isn't Fritz's idea, he doesn't know yet, I simply packed my things. – I don't think so. – I don't think he'll say all that much. It's all got too difficult for him, just in every day matters. – That's something we haven't arranged. – We just never talked about it, absolutely never. – No, he hasn't altered, on the contrary. – I'd be glad if you and Kurt could look after him a bit, to start with. – Yes, specially Sundays, and try to make him give up this flat. – It's too big for him. – I'd like to have come and said goodbye to you, but it's your porter, you know. – So, goodbye; no, don't come to the station, it's a bad idea. – Goodbye, I'll write. – That's a promise.

She hangs up without calling again. She has been smoking. Now she sets fire to the small book in which she has been looking up the numbers. She walks up and down two or three times. Then she starts speaking. She is rehearsing the short speech which she proposes to make to her husband. It is evident that he is sitting in a particular chair.

Well, Fritz, I'm off. I suppose I've waited too long, I'm awfully sorry, but . . .

She stands there thinking, then starts in a different way.

Fritz, you must let me go, you can't keep . . . I'll be your downfall, it's quite clear; I know you aren't a coward, you're not scared of the police, but there are worse things. They won't put you in a camp, but they'll ban you from the clinic any day now. You won't say anything at the time, but it'll make you ill. I'm not going to watch you sitting around in the flat pretending to read magazines, it's pure selfishness on my part, my leaving, that's all. Don't tell me anything . . .

She again stops. She makes a fresh start.

Don't tell me you haven't changed; you have! Only last week you established quite objectively that the proportion of Jewish scientists wasn't all that high. Objectivity is always the start of it, and why do you keep telling me I've never been such a Jewish chauvinist as now? Of course

I'm one. Chauvinism is catching. Oh, Fritz, what has happened to us?

She again stops. She makes a fresh start.

I never told you I wanted to go away, have done for a long time, because I can't talk when I look at you, Fritz. Then it seems to me there's no point in talking. It has all been settled already. What's got into them, d'you think? What do they really want? What am I doing to them? I've never had anything to do with politics. Did I vote Communist? But I'm just one of those bourgeois housewives with servants and so on, and now all of a sudden it seems only blondes can be that. I've often thought lately about something you told me years back, how some people were more valuable than others, so one lot were given insulin when they got diabetes and the others weren't. And this was something I understood, idiot that I was. Well, now they've drawn a new distinction of the same sort, and this time I'm one of the less valuable ones. Serves me right.

She again stops. She makes a fresh start.

Yes, I'm packing. Don't pretend you haven't noticed anything the last few days. Nothing really matters, Fritz, except just one thing: if we spend our last hour together without looking at each other's eyes. That's a triumph they can't be allowed, the liars who force everyone else to lie. Ten years ago when somebody said no one would think I was Jewish, you instantly said yes, they would. And that's fine. That was straightforward. Why take things in a roundabout way now? I'm packing so they shan't take away your job as senior physician. And because they've stopped saying good morning to you at the clinic, and because you're not sleeping nowadays. I don't want you to tell me I mustn't go. And I'm hurrying because I don't want to hear you telling me I must. It's a matter of time. Principles are a matter of time. They don't last for ever, any more than a glove does. There are good ones which last a long while. But even they only have a certain life. Don't get the idea that I'm angry. Yes, I am. Why should I always be understanding? What's wrong with the shape of my nose and the colour of my hair? I'm to leave the town where I was born just so they don't have to go short of butter. What sort of people are you, yourself included? You work out the quantum theory and the Trendelenburg test, then allow a lot of semi-barbarians to tell you you're to conquer the world but you can't have the woman you want. The artificial lung, and the dive-bomber! You are monsters or you pander to monsters. Yes, I know I'm being unreasonable, but what good is reason in a world like this? There you sit watching your wife pack and saying nothing. Walls have ears, is that it? But you people say nothing. One lot listens and the other keeps silent. To hell with that. I'm supposed to keep silent too. If I loved you I'd keep silent. I truly do love you. Give me those underclothes. They're suggestive. I'll need them. I'm thirty-six, that isn't too old, but I can't do much more experimenting. The next time I settle in a country things can't be like this. The next man I get must be allowed to keep me. And don't tell me you'll send me money; you know you won't be allowed to. And you aren't to pretend it's just a matter of four weeks either. This business is going to last rather more than four weeks. You know that, and so do I. So don't go telling me 'After all it's only for two or three weeks' as you hand me the fur coat I shan't need till next winter. And don't let's speak about disaster. Let's speak about disgrace. Oh, Fritz!

She stops. A door opens. She hurriedly sees to her appearance. The husband comes in.

THE HUSBAND: What are you doing? Tidying up?

THE WOMAN: No.

THE HUSBAND: Why are you packing?

THE WOMAN: I want to get away.

THE HUSBAND: What are you talking about?

THE WOMAN: We did mention the possibility of my going away for a bit. It's no longer very pleasant here.

THE HUSBAND: That's a lot of nonsense.

THE WOMAN: Do you want me to stay, then?

THE HUSBAND: Where are you thinking of going?

THE WOMAN: Amsterdam. Just away.

THE HUSBAND: But you've got nobody there.

THE WOMAN: No.

THE HUSBAND: Why don't you wish to stay here? There's absolutely no need for you to go so far as I'm concerned.

THE WOMAN: No.

THE HUSBAND: You know I haven't changed, you do, don't you, Judith?

THE WOMAN: Yes.

He embraces her. They stand without speaking among the suit-cases.

THE HUSBAND: And there's nothing else makes you want to go?

THE WOMAN: You know that.

THE HUSBAND: It might not be such a bad idea, I suppose. You need a breather. It's stifling in this place. I'll come and collect you. As soon as I get across the frontier, even if it's only for two days, I'll start feeling better.

THE WOMAN: Yes, why don't you?

THE HUSBAND: Things can't go on like this all that much longer. Something's bound to change. The whole business will die down again like an inflammation – it's a disaster, it really is.

THE WOMAN: Definitely. Did you run into Schöck?

THE HUSBAND: Yes, just on the stairs, that's to say. I think he's begun to be sorry about the way they dropped us. He was quite embarrassed. In the long run they can't completely sit on filthy intellectuals like us. And they won't be able to run a war with a lot of spineless wrecks. People aren't all that standoffish if you face up to them squarely. What time are you off, then?

THE WOMAN: Nine-fifteen.

THE HUSBAND: And where am I to send money to?

THE WOMAN: Let's say poste restante, Amsterdam main Post-Office.

THE HUSBAND: I'll see they give me a special permit. Good God, I can't send my wife off with ten marks a month. It's all a lousy business.

THE WOMAN: If you can come and collect me it'll do you a bit of good.

THE HUSBAND: To read a paper with something in it for once.

THE WOMAN: I rang Gertrud. She'll see you're all right.

THE HUSBAND: Quite unnecessary. For two or three weeks.

THE WOMAN *who has again begun packing:* Do you mind handing me my fur coat?

THE HUSBAND *handing it to her:* After all it's only for two or three weeks.

10

The spy

Here come the worthy schoolteachers
The Youth Movement takes the poor creatures
And makes them all thrust out their chest.
Every schoolboy's a spy. So now marking
Is based not on knowledge, but narking
And on who knows whose weaknesses best.

They educate traducers
To set hatchet-men and bruisers
On their own parents' tail.
Denounced by their sons as traitors
To Himmler's apparatus
The fathers go handcuffed to gaol.

Cologne 1935. A wet Sunday afternoon. The man, the wife and the boy have finished lunch. The maidservant enters.

THE MAIDSERVANT: Mr and Mrs Klimbtsch are asking if you are at home.

THE MAN *snarls:* No.

The maidservant goes out.

THE WIFE: You should have gone to the phone yourself. They must know we couldn't possibly have gone out yet.

THE MAN: Why couldn't we?

THE WIFE: Because it's raining.

THE MAN: That's no reason.

THE WIFE: Where could we have gone to? That's the first thing they'll ask.

THE MAN: Oh, masses of places.

THE WIFE: Let's go then.

THE MAN: Where to?

THE WIFE: If only it wasn't raining.

THE MAN: And where'd we go if it wasn't raining?

THE WIFE: At least in the old days you could go and meet someone.

Pause.

THE WIFE: It was a mistake you not going to the phone. Now they'll realise we don't want to have them.

THE MAN: Suppose they do?

THE WIFE: Then it wouldn't look very nice, our dropping them just when everyone else does.

THE MAN: We're not dropping them.

THE WIFE: Why shouldn't they come here in that case?

THE MAN: Because Klimbtsch bores me to tears.

THE WIFE: He never bored you in the old days.

THE MAN: In the old days ... All this talk of the old days gets me down.

THE WIFE: Well anyhow you'd never have cut him just because the school inspectors are after him.

THE MAN: Are you telling me I'm a coward?

Pause.

THE MAN: All right, ring up and tell them we've just come back on account of the rain.

The wife remains seated.

THE WIFE: What about asking the Lemkes to come over?

THE MAN: And have them go on telling us we're slack about civil defence?

THE WIFE *to the boy:* Klaus-Heinrich, stop fiddling with the wireless.

The boy turns his attention to the newspapers.

THE MAN: It's a disaster, its raining like this. It's quite intolerable, living in a country where it's a disaster when it rains.

THE WIFE: Do you really think it's sensible to go round making remarks like that?

THE MAN: I can make what remarks I like between my own four walls. This is my home, and I shall damn well say . . .

He is interrupted. The maidservant enters with coffee things. So long as she is present they remain silent.

THE MAN: Have we got to have a maid whose father is the block warden?

THE WIFE: We've been over that again and again. The last thing you said was that it had its advantages.

THE MAN: What aren't I supposed to have said? If you mentioned anything of the sort to your mother we could land in a proper mess.

THE WIFE: The things I talk about to my mother . . .

Enter the maidservant with the coffee.

THE WIFE: That's all right, Erna. You can go now, I'll see to it.

THE MAIDSERVANT: Thank you very much, ma'am.

THE BOY *looking up from his paper:* Is that how vicars always behave, dad?

THE MAN: How do you mean?

THE BOY: Like it says here.

THE MAN: What's that you're reading?

Snatches the paper from his hands.

THE BOY: Hey, our group leader said it was all right for us to know about anything in that paper.

THE MAN: I don't have to go by what your group leader says. It's for me to decide what you can or can't read.

THE WIFE: There's ten pfennigs, Klaus-Heinrich, run over and get yourself something.

THE BOY: But it's raining.

He hangs round the window, trying to make up his mind.

THE MAN: If they go on reporting these cases against priests I shall cancel the paper altogether.

THE WIFE: Which are you going to take, then? They're all reporting them.

THE MAN: If all the papers are full of this kind of filth I'd sooner not read a paper at all. And I wouldn't be any worse informed about what's going on in the world.

THE WIFE: There's something to be said for a bit of a clean-up.

THE MAN: Clean-up, indeed. The whole thing's politics.

THE WIFE: Well, it's none of our business anyway. After all, we're protestants.

THE MAN: It matters to our people all right if it can't hear the word vestry without being reminded of dirt like this.

THE WIFE: But what do you want them to do when this kind of thing happens?

THE MAN: What do I want them to do? Suppose they looked into their own back yard. I'm told it isn't all so snowy white in that Brown House of theirs.

THE WIFE: But that only goes to show how far our people's recovery has gone, Karl.

THE MAN: Recovery! A nice kind of recovery. If that's what recovery looks like, I'd sooner have the disease any day.

THE WIFE: You're so on edge today. Did something happen at the school?

THE MAN: What on earth could have happened at school? And for God's sake don't keep saying I'm on edge, it makes me feel on edge.

THE WIFE: We oughtn't to keep on quarrelling so, Karl. In the old days . . .

THE MAN: Just what I was waiting for. In the old days. Neither in the old days nor now did I wish to have my son's imagination perverted for him.

THE WIFE: Where has he got to, anyway?

THE MAN: How am I to know?

THE WIFE: Did you see him go?

THE MAN: No.

THE WIFE: I can't think where he can have gone. *She calls:* Klaus-Heinrich!

She hurries out of the room, and is heard calling. She returns.

THE WIFE: He really has left.

THE MAN: Why shouldn't he?

THE WIFE: But it's raining buckets.

THE MAN: Why are you so on edge at the boy's having left?

THE WIFE: You remember what we were talking about?

THE MAN: What's that got to do with it?

THE WIFE: You've been so careless lately.

THE MAN: I have certainly not been careless, but even if I had what's that got to do with the boy's having left?

THE WIFE: You know how they listen to everything.

THE MAN: Well?

THE WIFE: Well. Suppose he goes round telling people? You know how they're always dinning it into them in the Hitler Youth. They deliberately encourage the kids to repeat everything. It's so odd his going off so quietly.

THE MAN: Rubbish.

THE WIFE: Didn't you see when he went?

THE MAN: He was hanging round the window for quite a time.

THE WIFE: I'd like to know how much he heard.

THE MAN: But he must know what happens to people who get reported.

THE WIFE: What about that boy the Schmulkes were telling us about? They say his father's still in a concentration camp. I wish we knew how long he was in the room.

THE MAN: The whole thing's a load of rubbish.

He hastens to the other rooms and calls the boy.

THE WIFE: I just can't see him going off somewhere without saying a word. It wouldn't be like him.

THE MAN: Mightn't he be with a school friend?

THE WIFE: Then he'd have to be at the Mummermanns'. I'll give them a ring. (She telephones)

THE MAN: It's all a false alarm, if you ask me.

THE WIFE *telephoning:* Is that Mrs Mummermann? It's Mrs Furcke here. Good afternoon. Is Klaus-Heinrich with you? He isn't? – Then where on earth can the boy be? – Mrs Mummermann do you happen to know if the Hitler Youth place is open on Sunday afternoons? – It is? – Thanks a lot, I'll ask them.

She hangs up. They sit in silence.

THE MAN: What do you think he overheard?

THE WIFE: You were talking about the paper. You shouldn't have said what you did about the Brown House. He's so patriotic about that kind of thing.

THE MAN: What am I supposed to have said about the Brown House?

THE WIFE: You remember perfectly well. That things weren't all snowy white in there.

THE MAN: Well, nobody can take that as an attack, can they? Saying things aren't all white, or snowy white rather, as I qualified it — which makes a difference, quite a substantial one at that — well, it's more a kind of jocular remark like the man in the street makes in the vernacular, sort of, and all it really means is that probably not absolutely everything even there is always exactly as the Führer would like it to be. I quite deliberately emphasised that this was only 'probably' so by using the phrase, as I very well remember, 'I'm *told*' things aren't *all* — and that's another obvious qualification — so snowy white there. 'I'm told'; that doesn't mean its necessarily so. How could I say things aren't snowy white? I haven't any proof. Wherever there are human beings there are imperfections. That's all I was suggesting, and in very qualified form. And in any case there was a certain occasion when the Führer himself expressed the same kind of criticisms a great deal more strongly.

THE WIFE: I don't understand you. You don't need to talk to me in that way.

THE MAN: I'd like to think I don't. I wish I knew to what extent you gossip about all that's liable to be said between these four walls in the heat of the moment. Of course I wouldn't dream of accusing you of casting ill-considered aspersions on your husband, any more than I'd think my boy capable for one moment of doing anything to harm his own father. But doing harm and doing it wittingly are unfortunately two very different matters.

THE WIFE: You can stop that right now! What about the kind of things you say yourself? Here am I worrying myself silly whether you made that remark about life in Nazi Germany being intolerable before or after the one about the Brown House.

THE MAN: I never said anything of the sort.

THE WIFE: You're acting absolutely as if I were the police. All I'm doing is racking my brains about what the boy may have overheard.

THE MAN: The term Nazi Germany just isn't in my vocabulary.

THE WIFE: And that stuff about the warden of our block and how the papers print nothing but lies, and what you were saying about civil defence the other day – when does the boy hear a single constructive remark? That just doesn't do any good to a child's attitude of mind, it's simply demoralising, and at a time when the Führer keeps stressing that Germany's future lies in Germany's youth. He really isn't the kind of boy to rush off and denounce one just like that. It makes me feel quite ill.

THE MAN: He's vindictive, though.

THE WIFE: What on earth has he got to be vindictive about?

THE MAN: God knows, but there's bound to be something. The time I confiscated his tree-frog perhaps.

THE WIFE: But that was a week ago.

THE MAN: It's that kind of thing that sticks in his mind, though.

THE WIFE: What did you confiscate it for, anyway?

THE MAN: Because he wouldn't catch any flies for it. He was letting the creature starve.

THE WIFE: He really is run off his feet, you know.

THE MAN: There's not much the frog can do about that.

THE WIFE: But he never came back to the subject, and I gave him ten pfennigs only a moment ago. He only has to want something and he gets it.

THE MAN: Exactly. I call that bribery.

THE WIFE: What do you mean by that?

THE MAN: They'll simply say we were trying to bribe him to keep his mouth shut.

THE WIFE: What do you imagine they could do to you?

THE MAN: Absolutely anything. There's no limit. My God! And to think I'm supposed to be a teacher. An educator of our youth. Our youth scares me stiff.

THE WIFE: But they've nothing against you.

THE MAN: They've something against everyone. Everyone's suspect. Once the suspicion's there, one's suspect.

THE WIFE: But a child's not a reliable witness. A child hasn't the faintest idea what it's talking about.

THE MAN: So you say. But when did they start having to have witnesses for things?

THE WIFE: Couldn't we work out what you could have meant by your remarks? Then he could just have misunderstood you.

THE MAN: Well, what did I say? I can't even remember. It's all the fault of that damned rain. It puts one in a bad mood. Actually I'm the last person to say anything against the moral resurgence the German people is going through these days. I foresaw the whole thing as early as the winter of 1932.

THE WIFE: Karl, there just isn't time to discuss that now. We must straighten everything out right away. There's not a minute to spare.

THE MAN: I don't believe Karl-Heinrich's capable of it.

THE WIFE: Let's start with the Brown House and all the filth.

THE MAN: I never said a word about filth.

THE WIFE: You said the paper's full of filth and you want to cancel it.

THE MAN: Right, the paper. But not the Brown House.

THE WIFE: Couldn't you have been saying that you won't stand for such filth in the churches? And that you think the people now being tried could quite well be the same as used to spread malicious rumours about the Brown House suggesting things weren't all that snowy white there? And that they ought to have started looking into their own place instead? And what you were telling the boy was that he should stop fiddling with the wireless and read the paper because you're firmly of the opinion that the youth of the Third Reich should have a clear view of what's happening round about them.

THE MAN: It wouldn't be any use.

THE WIFE: Karl, you're not to give up now. You should be strong, like the Führer keeps on . . .

THE MAN: I'm not going to be brought before the law and have my own flesh and blood standing in the witness box and giving evidence against me.

THE WIFE: There's no need to take it like that.

THE MAN: It was a great mistake our seeing so much of the Klimbtsches.

THE WIFE: But nothing whatever has happened to him.

THE MAN: Yes, but there's talk of an inquiry.

THE WIFE: What would it be like if everybody got in such a panic as soon as there was talk of an inquiry?

THE MAN: Do you think our block warden has anything against us?

THE WIFE: You mean, supposing they asked him? He got a box of cigars for his birthday the other day and his Christmas box was ample.

THE MAN: The Gauffs gave him fifteen marks.

THE WIFE: Yes, but they were still taking a socialist paper in 1932, and as late as May 1933 they were hanging out the old nationalist flag.

The phone rings.

THE MAN: That's the phone.

THE WIFE: Shall I answer it?

THE MAN: I don't know.

THE WIFE: Who could be ringing us?

THE MAN: Wait a moment. If it rings again, answer it.

They wait. It doesn't ring again.

THE MAN: We can't go on living like this!

THE WIFE: Karl!

THE MAN: A Judas, that's what you've borne me. Sitting at the table listening, gulping down the soup we've given him and noting down whatever his father says, the little spy.

THE WIFE: That's a dreadful thing to say.

Pause.

THE WIFE: Do you think we ought to make any kind of preparations?

THE MAN: Do you think he'll bring them straight back with him?

THE WIFE: Could he really?

THE MAN: Perhaps I'd better put on my Iron Cross.

THE WIFE: Of course you must, Karl.

He gets it and puts it on with shaking hands.

THE WIFE: But they've nothing against you at school, have they?

THE MAN: How's one to tell? I'm prepared to teach what-ever they want taught; but what's that? If only I could tell . . . How am I to know what they want Bismarck to have been like? When they're taking so long to publish the new text books. Couldn't you give the maid another ten marks? She's another who's always listening.

THE WIFE *nodding:* And what about the picture of Hitler; shouldn't we hang it above your desk? It'd look better.

THE MAN: Yes, do that.

The wife starts taking down the picture.

THE MAN: Suppose the boy goes and says we deliberately rehung it, though, it might look as if we had a bad conscience.

The wife puts the picture back on its old hook.

THE MAN: Wasn't that the door?

THE WIFE: I didn't hear anything.

THE MAN: It was.

THE WIFE: Karl!

She embraces him.

THE MAN: Keep a grip on yourself. Pack some things for me.

The door of the flat opens. Man and wife stand rigidly side by side in the corner of the room. The door opens and enter the boy, a paper bag in his hand. Pause.

THE BOY: What's the matter with you people?

THE WIFE: Where have you been?

The boy shows her the bag, which contains chocolate.

THE WIFE: Did you simply go out to buy chocolate?

THE BOY: Wherever else? Obvious, isn't it?

He crosses the room munching, and goes out. His parents look enquiringly after him.

THE MAN: Do you suppose he's telling the truth?

The wife shrugs her shoulders.

11

The black shoes

> These widows and orphans you're seeing
> Have heard Him guaranteeing
> A great time by and by.
> Meanwhile they must make sacrifices
> As the shops all put up their prices.
> That great time is pie in the sky.

Bitterfeld, 1935. Kitchen in a working-class flat. The mother is peeling potatoes. Her thirteen-year-old daughter is doing homework.

THE DAUGHTER: Mum, am I getting my two pfennigs?

THE MOTHER: For the Hitler Youth?

THE DAUGHTER: Yes.

THE MOTHER: I haven't any money left.

THE DAUGHTER: But if I don't bring my two pfennigs a week I won't be going to the country this summer. And our teacher said Hitler wants town and country to get to know each other. Town people are supposed to get closer to the farmers. But I'll have to bring along my two pfennigs

THE MOTHER: I'll try to find some way of letting you have them.

THE DAUGHTER: Oh lovely, mum. I'll give a hand with the 'taters. It's lovely in the country, isn't it? Proper meals there. Our gym teacher was saying I've got a potato belly.

THE MOTHER: You've nothing of the kind.

THE DAUGHTER: Not right now. Last year I had. A bit.

THE MOTHER: I might be able to get us some offal.

THE DAUGHTER: I get my roll at school; that's more than you do. Bertha was saying when she went to the country last year they had bread and goose dripping. Meat too sometimes. Lovely, isn't it?

THE MOTHER: Of course.

THE DAUGHTER: And all that fresh air.

THE MOTHER: Didn't she have to do some work too?

THE DAUGHTER: Of course. But lots to eat. Only the farmer was a nuisance, she said.

THE MOTHER: What'd he do?

THE DAUGHTER: Oh, nothing. Just kept pestering her.

THE MOTHER: Aha.

THE DAUGHTER: Bertha's bigger than me, though. A year older.

THE MOTHER: Get on with your homework.

Pause, then:

THE DAUGHTER: But I won't have to wear those old black shoes from the welfare, will I?

THE MOTHER: You won't be needing them. You've got your other pair, haven't you?

THE DAUGHTER: Just that those have got a hole.

THE MOTHER: Oh dear, when it's so wet.

THE DAUGHTER: I'll put some paper in, that'll do it.

THE MOTHER: No, it won't. If they've gone they'll have to be resoled.

THE DAUGHTER: That's so expensive.

THE MOTHER: What've you got against the welfare pair?

THE DAUGHTER: I can't stand them.

THE MOTHER: Because they look so clumsy?

THE DAUGHTER: So you think so too.

THE MOTHER: Of course they're older.

THE DAUGHTER: Have I *got* to wear them?

THE MOTHER: If you can't stand them you needn't wear them.

THE DAUGHTER: I'm not being vain, am I?

THE MOTHER: No. Just growing up.

Pause, then:

THE DAUGHTER: Then can I have my two pfennigs, Mum? I do so want to go.

THE MOTHER *slowly:* I haven't the money for that.

12

Labour service

> By sweeping away class barriers
> The poor are made fetchers and carriers
> In Hitler's Labour Corps.
> The rich serve a year alongside them
> To show that no conflicts divide them.
> Some pay would please them more.

*The Lüneburger Heide, 1935. A Labour Service column at work.
A young worker and a student are digging together.*

THE STUDENT: What did they put that stocky little fellow
from Column 3 in clink for?

THE YOUNG WORKER *grinning:* The group leader was
saying we'll learn what it's like to work and he said, under
his breath like, he'd as soon learn what it's like to get a
pay packet. They weren't pleased.

THE STUDENT: Why say something like that?

THE YOUNG WORKER: Because he already knows what it's
like to work, I should think. He was down the pits at
fourteen.

THE STUDENT: Look out, Tubby's coming.

THE YOUNG WORKER: If he looks our way I can't just dig
out half a spit.

THE STUDENT: But I can't shovel away more than I'm doing.

THE YOUNG WORKER: If he cops me there'll be trouble.

THE STUDENT: No more cigarettes from me, then.

THE YOUNG WORKER: He'll cop me sure enough.

THE STUDENT: And you want to go on leave, don't you?
Think I'm going to pay you if you can't take a little risk
like that?

THE YOUNG WORKER: You've already had your money's
worth and more.

THE STUDENT: But I'm not going to pay you.

THE GROUP LEADER *comes and watches them:* Well, Herr Doktor, now you can see what working is really like, can't you?

THE STUDENT: Yes, Herr Group Leader.

The young worker digs half a spit of earth. The student pretends to be shovelling like mad.

THE GROUP LEADER: You owe it all to the Führer.

THE STUDENT: Yes, Herr Group Leader.

THE GROUP LEADER: Shoulder to shoulder and no class barriers; that's his way. The Führer wants no distinctions made in his labour camps. Never mind who your dad is. Carry on! *He goes.*

THE STUDENT: I don't call that half a spit.

THE YOUNG WORKER: Well, I do.

THE STUDENT: No cigarettes for today. Better remember there are an awful lot of people want cigarettes just as much as you.

THE YOUNG WORKER *slowly:* Yes, there are an awful lot of people like me. That's something we often forget.

13

Workers' playtime

Then the media, a travelling circus
Come to interview the workers
With microphone in hand
But the workers can't be trusted
So the interview is adjusted
To fit what Goebbels has planned.

Leipzig 1934. Foreman's office in a factory. A radio announcer bearing a microphone is chatting to three workers; a middle-aged worker, an old worker and a woman worker. In the background are a gentleman from the office and a stocky figure in SA uniform.

THE ANNOUNCER: Here we are with flywheels and driving belts in full swing all around us, surrounded by our comrades working as busily as ants, joyously doing their bit to provide our beloved fatherland with everything it requires. This morning we are visiting the Fuchs spinning mills. And in spite of the hard toil and the tensing of every muscle here we see nothing but joyous and contented faces on all sides. But let us get our comrades to speak for themselves. (To the old worker) I understand you've been working here for twenty-one years, Mr . . .

THE OLD WORKER: Sedelmaier.

THE ANNOUNCER: Mr Sedelmaier. Tell me, Mr Sedelmaier, how is it that we see nothing but these happy, joyous faces in every side?

THE OLD WORKER *after a moment's thought:* There's a lot of jokes told.

THE ANNOUNCER: Really? Right, so a cheerful jest or two makes work seem child's play, what? The deadly menace of pessimism is unknown under National Socialism, you mean. Different in the old days, wasn't it?

THE OLD WORKER: Aye.

THE ANNOUNCER: That rotten old Weimar republic didn't give the workers much to laugh about you mean. What are we working for, they used to ask.

THE OLD WORKER: Aye, that's what some of them say.

THE ANNOUNCER: I didn't quite get that. Oh, I see, you're referring to the inevitable grouses, but they're dying out now they see that kind of thing's a waste of time because everything's booming in the Third Reich now there's a strong hand on the helm once again. That's what you feel too, – *to the woman worker* – isn't it, Miss . . .

THE WOMAN WORKER: Schmidt.

THE ANNOUNCER: Miss Schmidt. And which of these steel mammoths enjoys your services?

THE WOMAN WORKER *reciting:* And then we also work at decorating our place of work which gives us great pleasure. Our portrait of the Führer was purchased thanks to voluntary contributions and we are very proud of him. Also of the geranium plants which provide a magical touch of colour in the greyness of our working environment, by suggestion of Miss Kinze.

THE ANNOUNCER: So you decorate your place of work with flowers, the sweet offspring of the fields. And I imagine there've been a good few other changes in this factory since Germany's destiny took its new turning?

GENTLEMAN FROM THE OFFICE *prompting:* Wash rooms.

THE WOMAN WORKER: The wash rooms were the personal idea of Mr Bäuschle our managing director for which we would like to express our heartfelt thanks. Anybody who wants to wash can do so in these fine washrooms so long as there isn't too much of a crowd fighting for the basins.

THE ANNOUNCER: Everybody wants to be first, what? So there's always a jolly throng?

THE WOMAN WORKER: Only six taps for 552 of us. So there are lots of quarrels. It's disgraceful how some of them behave.

THE ANNOUNCER: But it's all sorted out perfectly happily. And now we are going to hear a few words from Mr — if you'd be so good as to tell me your name?

THE WORKER: Mahn.

THE ANNOUNCER: Mr Mahn. Right, Mr Mahn, would you tell us what moral effect the great increase in the workforce here has had on your fellow workers?

THE WORKER: How do you mean?

THE ANNOUNCER: Well, are all of you happy to see the wheels turning and plenty of work for everybody?

THE WORKER: You bet.

THE ANNOUNCER: And everybody once more able to take his wage packet home at the end of the week, that's not to be sneezed at either.

THE WORKER: No.

THE ANNOUNCER: Things weren't always like that. Under that rotten old republic many a comrade had to plod his weary way to the public welfare and live on charity.

THE WORKER: 18 marks 50. No deductions.

THE ANNOUNCER *with a forced laugh:* Ha. Ha. A capital joke! Not much to deduct, was there?

THE WORKER: No. Nowadays they deduct more.

The gentleman from the office moves forward uneasily, as does the stocky man in SA uniform.

THE ANNOUNCER: So there we are, everybody's once again got bread and work under National Socialism. You're absolutely right, Mr – what did you say your name was? Not a single wheel is idle, not a single shaft needs to rust up in Adolf Hitler's Germany. *He roughly pushes the worker away from the microphone.* In joyful cooperation the intellectual worker and the manual worker are tackling the reconstruction of our beloved German Fatherland. Heil Hitler!

14

The box

> The coffins the SA carry
> Are sealed up tight, to bury
> Their victims' raw remains.
> Here's one who wouldn't give in
> He fought for better living
> That we might lose our chains.

Essen 1934. Working-class flat. A woman with two children. A young worker and his wife, who are calling on them. The woman is weeping. Steps can be heard on the staircase. The door is open.

THE WOMAN: He simply said they were paying starvation wages, that's all. And it's true. What's more, our elder girl's got lung trouble and we can't afford milk. They couldn't possibly have harmed him, could they?
The SA men bring in a big box and put it on the floor.
SA MAN: Don't make a song and dance about it. Anybody can catch pneumonia. Here are the papers, all present and correct. And don't you go doing anything silly, now.

The S A men leave.

A CHILD: Mum, is dad in there?

THE WORKER *who has gone over to the box:* That's zinc it's made of.

THE CHILD: Please can we open it?

THE WORKER *in a rage:* You bet we can. Where's your toolbox?

THE YOUNG WOMAN: Don't you open it, Hans. It'll only make them come for you.

THE WORKER: I want to see what they did to him. They're frightened of people seeing that. That's why they used zinc. Leave me alone!

THE YOUNG WOMAN: I'm not leaving you alone. Didn't you hear them?

THE WORKER: Don't you think we ought to just have a look at him?

THE WOMAN *taking her children by the hand and going up to the zinc box:* There's still my brother, they might come for him, Hans. And they might come for you too. The box can stay shut. We don't need to see him. He won't be forgotten.

15

Release

> Questioned in torture cellars
> These men were no tale-tellers.
> They held out all through the night.
> Let's hope they didn't go under
> But their wives and friends must wonder
> What took place at first light.

Berlin, 1936. Working-class kitchen. Sunday morning. Man and wife. Sound of military music in the distance.

THE MAN: He'll be here any minute.

THE WIFE: None of you know anything against him, after all.

THE MAN: All we know is that they let him out of the concentration camp.

THE WIFE: So why don't you trust him?

THE MAN: There've been too many cases. They put so much pressure on them in there.

THE WIFE: How's he to convince you?

THE MAN: We'll find out where he stands all right.

THE WIFE: Might take time.

THE MAN: Yes.

THE WIFE: And he might be a first-rate comrade.

THE MAN: He might.

THE WIFE: It must be dreadful for him when he sees everybody mistrusting him.

THE MAN: He knows it's necessary.

THE WIFE: All the same.

THE MAN: I can hear something. Don't go away while we're talking.

There is a ring. The man opens the door, the released man enters.

THE MAN: Hullo, Max.

The released man silently shakes hands with the man and his wife.

THE WIFE: Would you like a cup of coffee with us? We're just going to have some.

THE RELEASED MAN: If it's not too much trouble.

Pause.

THE RELEASED MAN: You got a new cupboard.

THE WIFE: It's really an old one, cost eleven marks fifty. Ours was falling to pieces.

THE RELEASED MAN: Ha.

THE MAN: Anything doing in the street?

THE RELEASED MAN: They're collecting.

THE WIFE: We could do with a suit for Willi.

THE MAN: Hey, I'm not out of work.

THE WIFE: That's just why we could do with a suit for you.

THE MAN: Don't talk such nonsense.

THE RELEASED MAN: Work or no work, anybody can do with something.

THE MAN: You found work yet?

THE RELEASED MAN: They say so.

THE MAN: At Siemens?

THE RELEASED MAN: There or some other place.

THE MAN: It's not as hard as it was.

THE RELEASED MAN: No.

Pause.

THE MAN: How long you been inside?

THE RELEASED MAN: Six months

THE MAN: Meet anyone in there?

THE RELEASED MAN: No one I knew. *Pause.* They're sending them to different camps these days. You could land up in Bavaria.

THE MAN: Ha.

THE RELEASED MAN: Things haven't changed much outside.

THE MAN: Not so as you'd notice.

THE WIFE: We live a very quiet life, you know. Willi hardly ever sees any of his old friends, do you, Willi?

THE MAN: Ay, we keep pretty much to ourselves.

THE RELEASED MAN: I don't suppose you ever got them to shift those rubbish bins from the hallway?

THE WIFE: Goodness, you remember that? Ay, he says he can't find anywhere else for them.

THE RELEASED MAN *as the wife is pouring him a cup of coffee:* Just give me a drop. I don't want to stay long.

THE MAN: Got any plans?

THE RELEASED MAN: Selma told me you looked after her when she was laid up. Thanks very much.

THE WIFE: It was nothing. We'd have told her to come over in the evening more, only we've not even got the wireless.

THE MAN: Anything they tell you is in the paper anyway.

THE RELEASED MAN: Not that there's much in the old rag.

THE WIFE: As much as there is in the *Völkischer Beobachter*, though.

THE RELEASED MAN: And in the *Völkischer Beobachter* there's just as much as there is in the old rag, eh?

THE MAN: I don't read that much in the evenings. Too tired.

THE WIFE: Here, what's wrong with your hand? All screwed up like that and two fingers missing?

THE RELEASED MAN: Oh, I had a fall.

THE MAN: Good thing it was your left one.

THE RELEASED MAN: Ay, that was a bit of luck. I'd like a word with you. No offence meant, Mrs Mahn.

THE WIFE: None taken. I've just got to clean the stove.

She gets to work on the stove. The released man watches her, a thin smile on his lips.

THE MAN: We've got to go out right after dinner. Has Selma quite recovered?

THE RELEASED MAN: All but for her hip. Doing washing is bad for her. Tell me . . . *He stops short and looks at them. They look at him. He says nothing further.*

THE MAN *hoarsely:* What about a walk round the Alexanderplatz before dinner? See what's doing with their collection?

THE WIFE: We could do that, couldn't we?

THE RELEASED MAN: Sure.

Pause.

THE RELEASED MAN *quietly:* Hey, Willi, you know I've not changed.

THE MAN *lightly:* Course you haven't. They might have a band playing there. Get yourself ready, Anna. We've finished our coffee. I'll just run a comb through my hair.

They go into the next room. The released man remains seated. He has picked up his hat. He is aimlessly whistling. The couple return, dressed to go out.

THE MAN: Come on then, Max.

THE RELEASED MAN: Very well. But let me just say: I find it entirely right.

THE MAN: Good, then let's go.

They go out together.

16

Charity begins at home

With banners and loud drumming
The Winter Aid come slumming
Into the humblest door.
They've marched round and collected
The crumbs the rich have rejected
And brought them to the poor.

Their hands, more used to beatings
Now offer gifts and greetings.
They conjure up a smile.
Their charity soon crashes
Their food all turns to ashes
And chokes the uttered 'Heil!'

Karlsruhe 1937. An old woman's flat. She is standing at a table with her daughter while the two SA men deliver a parcel from the Winter Aid Organisation.

THE FIRST SA MAN: Here you are, Ma, a present from the Führer.

THE SECOND SA MAN: So you can't say he's not looking after you properly.

THE OLD WOMAN: Thanks very much, thanks very much. Look, Erna, potatoes. And a woollen sweater. And apples.

THE FIRST SA MAN: And a letter from the Führer with something in it. Go on, open it.

THE OLD WOMAN *opening the letter:* Five marks! What d'you say to that, Erna?

THE SECOND SA MAN: Winter Aid.

THE OLD WOMAN: You must take an apple, young man, and you too, for bringing these things to me, and up all those stairs too. It's all I got to offer you. And I'll take one myself.

She takes a bite at an apple. All eat apples with the exception of the young woman.

THE OLD WOMAN: Go on, Erna, you take one too, don't just stand there. That shows you things aren't like your husband says.

THE FIRST SA MAN: What does he say, then?

THE YOUNG WOMAN: He doesn't say anything. The old lady's wandering.

THE OLD WOMAN: Of course it's just his way of talking, you know, it don't mean any harm, just the way they all talk. How prices have gone up a bit much lately. *Pointing at her daughter with the apple:* And she got her account book and actually reckoned food had cost her 123 marks more this year than last. Didn't you, Erna? *She notices that the SA man seems to have taken this amiss.* But of course it's just because we're rearming, isn't it? What's the matter, I said something wrong?

THE FIRST SA MAN: Where do you keep your account book, young woman?

THE SECOND SA MAN: And who are you in the habit of showing it to?

THE YOUNG WOMAN: It's at home. I don't show it to no one.

THE OLD WOMAN: You can't object if she keeps accounts, how could you?

THE FIRST SA MAN: And if she goes about spreading alarm and despondency; are we allowed to object then?

THE SECOND SA MAN: What's more I don't remember her saying 'Heil Hitler' all that loudly when we came in. Do you?

THE OLD WOMAN: But she *did* say 'Heil Hitler' and I say the same. 'Heil Hitler'!

THE SECOND SA MAN: Nice nest of Marxists we've stumbled on here, Albert. We'd better have a good look at those accounts. Just you come along and show us where you live.

He seizes the young woman by the arm.

THE OLD WOMAN: But she's in her third month. You can't ... that's no way for you to behave. After bring-

ing the parcel and taking the apples. Erna! But she *did*
say 'Heil Hitler', what am I to do, Heil Hitler! Heil
Hitler!

She vomits up the apple. The SA lead her daughter off.

THE OLD WOMAN *continuing to vomit:* Heil Hitler!

17

Two bakers

> Now come the master bakers
> Compelled to act as fakers
> And made to use their art
> On substitute ingredients –
> Spuds, bran and blind obedience.
> It lands them in the cart.

*Landsberg, 1936. Prison yard. Prisoners are walking in a circle.
Now and again two of them talk quietly to each other downstage.*

THE ONE: So you're a baker too, new boy?

THE OTHER: Yes. Are you?

THE ONE: Yes. What did they get you for?

THE OTHER: Look out!

They again walk round the circle.

THE OTHER: Refusing to mix potatoes and bran in my
bread. And you? How long've you been in?

THE ONE: Two years.

THE OTHER: And what did they get you for? Look out!

They again walk round the circle.

THE ONE: Mixing bran in my bread. Two years ago they
still called that adulteration.

THE OTHER: Look out!

18

The farmer feeds his sow

> You'll notice in our procession
> The farmer's sour expression:
> They've underpriced his crop.
> But what his pigs require
> Is milk, whose price has gone higher.
> It makes him blow his top.

*Aichach, 1937. A farmyard. It is night. The farmer is standing by
the pigsty giving instructions to his wife and two children.*

THE FARMER: I wasn't having you mixed up in this, but
you found out and now you'll just have to shut your trap.
Or else your Dad'll go off to Landsberg gaol for the rest
of his born days. There's nowt wrong in our feeding our
cattle when they're hungry. God doesn't want any beast
to starve. And soon as she's hungry she squeals and I'm
not having a sow squealing with hunger on my farm. But
they won't let me feed her. Cause the State says so. But
I'm feeding her just the same, I am. Cause if I don't feed
her she'll die on me, and I shan't get any compensation
for that.

THE FARMER'S WIFE: Too right. Our grain's our grain.
And those buggers have no business telling us what to
do. They got the Jews out but the State's the worst Jew
of them all. And the Reverend Father saying 'Thou shalt
not muzzle the ox that treadeth out the corn.' That's his
way of telling us go ahead and feed our cattle. It weren't
us as made their four year plan, and we weren't asked.

THE FARMER: That's right. They don't favour the farmers
and the farmers don't favour them. I'm supposed to deliver over my grain and pay through the nose for my
cattle feed. So that that spiv can buy guns.

THE FARMER'S WIFE: You stand by the gate, Toni, and

you, Marie, run into the pasture and soon as you see anyone coming give us a call.

The children take up their positions. The farmer mixes his pig-swill and carries it to the sty, looking cautiously around him. His wife looks cautiously too.

THE FARMER *pouring the swill into the sow's trough:* Go on, have a good feed, love. Heil Hitler! When a beast's hungry there ain't no State.

19

The old militant

Behold several million electors.
One hundred per cent in all sectors
Have asked to be led by the nose.
They didn't get real bread and butter
They didn't get warm coats or fodder
They *did* get the leader they chose.

Calw (Württemberg), 1938. A square with small shops. In the background a butcher's, in the foreground a dairy It is a dark winter's morning. The butcher's is not open yet. But the dairy's lights are on and there a few customers waiting.

A PETIT-BOURGEOIS: No butter again today, what?

THE WOMAN: It'll be all I can afford on my old man's pay, anyway.

A YOUNG FELLOW: Stop grumbling, will you? Germany needs guns, not butter, no question about that. He spelled it out.

THE WOMAN *backing down:* Quite right too.

Silence.

THE YOUNG FELLOW: D'you think we could have reoc-cupied the Rhineland with butter? Everyone was for doing it the way we did, but catch them making any sacrifices.

A SECOND WOMAN: Keep your hair on. All of us are making some.

THE YOUNG FELLOW *mistrustfully:* What d'you mean?

THE SECOND WOMAN *to the first:* Don't you give something when they come round collecting?

The first woman nods.

THE SECOND WOMAN: There you are. She's giving. And so are we. Voluntary-like.

THE YOUNG FELLOW: That's an old story. Not a penny to spare when the Führer needs a bit of backing, as it were, for his mighty tasks. It's just rags, what they give the Winder Aid. They'd give'em the moths if they could get away with it. We know the kind we got to deal with. That factory owner in number twelve went and gave us a pair of worn out riding boots.

THE PETIT-BOURGEOIS: No foresight, that's the trouble.

The dairywoman comes out of her shop in a white apron.

THE DAIRYWOMAN: Won't be long now. *To the second woman:* Morning, Mrs Ruhl. Did you hear they came for young Lettner last night?

THE SECOND WOMAN: What, the butcher?

THE DAIRYWOMAN: Right, his son.

THE SECOND WOMAN: But he was in the SA.

THE DAIRYWOMAN: Used to be. The old fellow's been in the party since 1929. He was away at a livestock sale yesterday or they'd have taken him off too.

THE SECOND WOMAN: What're they supposed to have done?

THE DAIRYWOMAN: Been overcharging for meat. He was hardly getting nothing on his quota and had to turn customers away. Then they say he started buying on the black market. From the Jews even.

THE YOUNG FELLOW: Bound to come for him, weren't they?

THE DAIRYWOMAN: Used to be one of the keenest of the lot, he did. He shopped old Zeisler at number seventeen for not taking the *Völkischer Beobachter.* An old militant, that's him.

THE SECOND WOMAN: He'll get a surprise when he comes back.

THE DAIRYWOMAN: *If* he comes back.

THE PETIT-BOURGEOIS: No foresight, that's the trouble.

THE SECOND WOMAN: Looks as if they won't open at all today.

THE DAIRYWOMAN: Best thing they can do. The police only have to look round a place like that and they're bound to find something, aren't they? With stock so hard to get. We get ours from the cooperative, no worries so far. *Calling out:* There'll be no cream today. *General murmur of disappointment.* They say Lettners raised a mortgage on the house. They counted on its being cancelled or something.

THE PETIT-BOURGEOIS: They can't start cancelling mortgages. That'd be going a bit too far.

THE SECOND WOMAN: Young Lettner was quite a nice fellow.

THE DAIRYWOMAN: Old Lettner was always the crazy one. Went and shoved the boy in the SA, just like that. When he'd sooner have been going out with a girl, if you ask me.

THE YOUNG FELLOW: What d'you mean, crazy?

THE DAIRYWOMAN: Crazy, did I say? Oh, he always went crazy if anyone said anything against the Idea, in the old days. He was always speaking about the Idea, and down with the selfishness of the individual.

THE PETIT-BOURGEOIS: They're opening up after all.

THE SECOND WOMAN: Got to live, haven't they?

A stout woman comes out of the butcher's shop, which is now half-lit. She stops on the pavement and looks down the street for something. Then she turns to the diary woman.

THE BUTCHER'S WIFE: Good morning, Mrs Schlichter. Have you seen our Richard? He should have been here with the meat well before now.

The dairywoman doesn't reply. All of them just stare at her. She understands, and goes quickly back into the shop.

THE DAIRYWOMAN: Act as though nothing's happened. It all blew up day before yesterday when the old man made

such a stink you could hear him shouting right across the
square. They counted that against him.

THE SECOND WOMAN: I never heard a word about that,
Mrs Schlichter.

THE DAIRYWOMAN: Really? Didn't you know how he
refused to hang that plaster ham they brought him in his
shop window? He'd gone and ordered it cause they in-
sisted, what with him hanging nothing in his window all
week but the slate with the prices. He said: I've got nothing left for the window. When they brought that dummy
ham, along with a side of veal, what's more, so natural
you'd think it was real, he shouted he wasn't hanging any
make-believe stuff in his window as well as a lot more I
wouldn't care to repeat. Against the government, all of it,
after which threw the stuff into the road. They had to
pick it up out of the dirt.

THE SECOND WOMAN: Ts, ts, ts, ts.

THE PETIT-BOURGEOIS: No foresight, that's the trouble.

THE SECOND WOMAN: How can people lose control like
that?

THE DAIRYWOMAN: Particularly such a smooth operator.
*At this moment someone turns on a second light in the butcher's
shop.*

THE DAIRYWOMAN: Look at that!
She points excitedly at the half-lit shop window.

THE SECOND WOMAN: There's something in the window.

THE DAIRYWOMAN: It's old Lettner. In his coat too. But
what's he standing on? *Suddenly calls out:* Mrs Lettner!

THE BUTCHER'S WIFE: What is it?
*The dairywoman points speechlessly at the shop window. The
butcher's wife glances at it, screams and falls down in a faint.
The second woman and the dairywoman hurry over to her.*

THE SECOND WOMAN *back over her shoulder:* He's hung
himself in his shop window.

THE PETIT-BOURGEOIS: There's a sign round his neck.

THE FIRST WOMAN: It's the slate. There's something
written on it.

THE SECOND WOMAN: It says 'I voted for Hitler'.

20

The Sermon on the Mount

The Church's Ten Commandments
Are subject to amendments
By order of the police.
Her broken head is bleeding
For new gods are succeeding
Her Jewish god of peace

Lübeck 1937. A fisherman's kitchen. The fisherman is dying. By his bed stand his wife and, in SA uniform, his son. The pastor is there.

THE DYING MAN: Tell me: is there really anything afterwards?

THE PASTOR: Are you then troubled by doubts?

THE WIFE: He's kept on saying these last four days that there's so much talking and promising you don't know what to believe. You mustn't think badly of him, your Reverence.

THE PASTOR: Afterwards cometh eternal life.

THE DYING MAN: And that'll be better?

THE PASTOR: Yes.

THE DYING MAN: It's got to be.

THE WIFE: He's taken it out of himself, you know.

THE PASTOR: Believe me, God knows it.

THE DYING MAN: You think so? *After a pause:* Up there, I suppose a man'll be able to open his mouth for once now and again?

THE PASTOR *slightly confused:* It is written that faith moveth mountains. You must believe. You will find it easier then.

THE WIFE: Your Reverence, you mustn't think he doesn't believe. He always took Communion. *To her husband, urgently:* Here's his Reverence thinking you don't believe. But you do believe, don't you?

THE DYING MAN: Yes . . .
Silence.

THE DYING MAN: There's nothing else then.

THE PASTOR: What are you trying to say by that? There's nothing else then?

THE DYING MAN: Just; there's nothing else then. Eh? I mean, suppose there had been anything?

THE PASTOR: But what could there have been?

THE DYING MAN: Anything at all.

THE PASTOR: But you have had your dear wife and your son.

THE WIFE: You had us, didn't you?

THE DYING MAN: Yes . . .
Silence.

THE DYING MAN: I mean: if life had added up to anything . . .

THE PASTOR: I'm not quite sure I understand you. You surely don't mean that you only believe because your life has been all toil and hardship?

THE DYING MAN *looks round until he catches sight of his son:* And is it going to be better for them?

THE PASTOR: For youth, you mean? Let us hope so.

THE DYING MAN: If the boat had had a motor . . .

THE WIFE: You mustn't worry about that now.

THE PASTOR: It is not a moment to be thinking of such things.

THE DYING MAN: I've got to.

THE WIFE: We'll manage all right.

THE DYING MAN: But suppose there's a war?

THE WIFE: Don't speak about that now. *To the pastor:* These last times he was always talking to the boy about war. They didn't agree about it.
The pastor looks at the son.

THE SON: He doesn't believe in our future.

THE DYING MAN: Tell me: up there, does *he* want war?

THE PASTOR *hesitating:* It says: Blessed are the peacemakers.

THE DYING MAN: But if there's a war . . .

THE SON: The Führer doesn't want a war!
The dying man makes a wide gesture of the hand, as if shoving that away.

THE DYING MAN: So if there's a war . . .

The son wants to say something.

THE WIFE: Keep quiet now.

THE DYING MAN *to the pastor, pointing at his son:* You tell him that about the peacemakers.

THE PASTOR: We are all in the hand of God, you must not forget.

THE DYING MAN: You telling him?

THE WIFE: But his Reverence can't do anything to stop war, be reasonable. Better not talk about it nowadays, eh, your Reverence?

THE DYING MAN: You know: they're a swindling lot. I can't buy a motor for my boat. Their aeroplanes get motors all right. For war, for killing. And when it's stormy like this I can't bring her in because I haven't a motor. Those swindlers! War's what they're after! *He sinks back exhausted.*

THE WIFE *anxiously fetches a cloth and a bowl of water, and wipes away his sweat:* You mustn't listen. He doesn't know what he's saying.

THE PASTOR: You should calm yourself, Mr Claasen.

THE DYING MAN: You telling him about the peacemakers?

THE PASTOR *after a pause:* He can read for himself. It's in the Sermon on the Mount.

THE DYING MAN: He says it's all written by a Jew and it doesn't apply.

THE WIFE: Don't start on that again! He doesn't mean it like that. That's what he hears the others saying.

THE DYING MAN: Yes. *To the Pastor:* Does it apply?

THE WIFE *with an anxious glance at her son:* Don't make trouble for his Reverence, Hannes. You shouldn't ask that.

THE SON: Why shouldn't he ask that?

THE DYING MAN: Does it apply or not?

THE PASTOR: It is also written: Render therefore unto Caesar the things which are Caesar's; and unto God the things that are God's.

The dying man sinks back. His wife lays the damp cloth on his forehead.

21

The motto

> Their boys learn it's morally healthy
> To lay down one's life for the wealthy:
> It's a lesson that's made very clear.
> It's far harder than spelling or figures
> But their teachers are terrible floggers
> So they're fearful of showing fear.

Chemnitz, 1937. Meeting room of the Hitler Youth. A squad of boys, mostly with gas masks slung round their necks. A small group are looking at a boy with no mask who is sitting by himself on a bench and helplessly moving his lips as if learning something.

THE FIRST BOY: He still hasn't got one.

THE SECOND BOY: His old lady won't buy him one.

THE FIRST BOY: But she must know he'll get into trouble.

THE THIRD BOY: If she ain't got the cash . . .

THE FIRST BOY: And old Fatty's got a down on him in any case.

THE SECOND BOY: He's back to learning it: 'The Motto'.

THE FOURTH BOY: That's four weeks he's been trying to learn it, and it's just a couple of verses.

THE THIRD BOY: He's known it off for ages.

THE SECOND BOY: He only gets stuck cause he's frightened.

THE FOURTH BOY: That's terribly funny, don't you think?

THE FIRST BOY: Devastating. *He calls:* D'you know it, Pschierer?

> *The fifth boy looks up, distracted, gets the meaning and nods. Then he goes on learning.*

THE SECOND BOY: Old Fatty only keeps on at him cause he's got no gasmask

THE THIRD BOY: The way he tells it, it's because he wouldn't go to the pictures with him.

THE FOURTH BOY: That's what I heard too. D'you think it's true?

THE SECOND BOY: Could be, why not? I wouldn't go to the pictures with Fatty either. But he wouldn't start anything with me. My old man wouldn't half kick up a stink.

THE FIRST BOY: Look out, here's Fatty.

The boys come to attention in two ranks. Enter a somewhat corpulent Scharführer. The Hitler salute.

THE SCHARFÜHRER: From the right, number!

They number.

THE SCHARFÜHRER: Gasmasks – on!

The boys put on their gasmasks. Some of them have not got one. They simply go through the motions of the drill.

THE SCHARFÜHRER: We'll start with 'The Motto'. Who's going to recite it for us? *He looks round as if unable to make up his mind, then suddenly:* Pschierer! You do it so nicely.

The fifth boy steps forward and stands to attention in front of the others.

THE SCHARFÜHRER: Can you do it, maestro?

THE FIFTH BOY: Yes, sir!

THE SCHARFÜHRER: Right, get cracking! Verse number one!

THE FIFTH BOY:

Thou shalt gaze on death unblinking –
Saith the motto for our age –
Sent into the fray unflinching
Heedless of the battle's rage.

THE SCHARFÜHRER: Don't wet your pants now. Carry on! Verse number two!

THE FIFTH BOY:

Victory is ours for gaining.
Beat, stab, shoot . . .

He has got stuck, and repeats these words. One or two of the boys find it difficult not to burst out laughing.

THE SCHARFÜHRER: So once again you haven't learnt it?

THE FIFTH BOY: Yes, sir!

THE SCHARFÜHRER: I bet you learn something different at home, don't you? *Shouts:* Carry on!

THE FIFTH BOY:

Beat, stab, shoot them so they fall.
Be a German . . . uncomplaining, uncomplaining
Be a German uncomplaining
Die for this . . . die for this, and give your all.

THE SCHARFÜHRER: Now what's so difficult about that?

22

News of the bombardment of Almeria gets to the barracks

The soldiers in His armed forces
Get full meat and pudding courses
And can also ask for more.
It helps them to face the firing
And not to think of enquiring
Who He is fighting for.

Berlin, 1937. Corridor in a barracks. Looking around them nervously, two working class boys are carrying away something wrapped in brown paper.

THE FIRST BOY: Aren't half worked up today, are they?

THE SECOND BOY: They say it's cause war could break out. Over Spain.

THE FIRST BOY: White as a sheet, some of them.

THE SECOND BOY: Cause we bombarded Almeria. Last night.

THE FIRST BOY: Where's that?

THE SECOND BOY: In Spain, silly. Hitler telegraphed for a German warship to bombard Almeria right away. As a punishment. Cause they're reds down there, and reds have got to be scared shitless of the Third Reich. Now it could lead to war.

THE FIRST BOY: And now they're scared shitless too.

THE SECOND BOY: Right. Scared shitless, that's them.

THE FIRST BOY: What do they want to go bombarding for if they're white as a sheet and scared shitless cause it could lead to war?

THE SECOND BOY: They just started bombarding cause Hitler wants it that way.

THE FIRST BOY: Whatever Hitler wants they want too. The whole lot are for Hitler. Cause he's built up our new armed forces.

THE SECOND BOY: You got it.
Pause.

THE FIRST BOY: Think we can sneak out now?

THE SECOND BOY: Better wait, or we'll run into one of those Lieutenants. Then he'll confiscate everything and they'll be in trouble.

THE FIRST BOY: Decent of them to let us come every day.

THE SECOND BOY: Oh, they ain't millionaires any more than us, you know. They know how it is. My old lady only gets ten marks a week, and there are three of us. It's just enough for potatoes.

THE FIRST BOY: Smashing nosh they get here. Meatballs today.

THE SECOND BOY: How much d'they give you this time?

THE FIRST BOY: One dollop, as usual. Why?

THE SECOND BOY: They gave me two this time.

THE FIRST BOY: Let's see. They only gave one.
The second boy shows him.

THE FIRST BOY: Did you say anything to them?

THE SECOND BOY: No. Just 'good morning' as usual.

THE FIRST BOY: I don't get it. And me too, 'Heil Hitler' as usual.

THE SECOND BOY: Funny. They gave me two dollops.

THE FIRST BOY: Why d'they suddenly do that. I don't get it.

THE SECOND BOY: Nor me. Coast's clear now.
They quickly run off.

23

Job creation

> He sees that jobs are provided.
> The poor go where they are guided:
> He likes them to be keen.
> They're allowed to serve the nation.
> Their blood and perspiration
> Can fuel His war machine.

Spandau, 1937. A worker comes home and finds a neighbour there.

THE NEIGHBOUR: Good evening, Mr Fenn. I just came to see if your wife could lend me some bread. She's popped out for a moment.

THE MAN: That's all right, Mrs Dietz. What d'you think of the job I got?

THE NEIGHBOUR: Ah, they're all getting work. At the new factory, aren't you? You'll be turning out bombers then?

THE MAN: And how.

THE NEIGHBOUR: They'll be needed in Spain these days.

THE MAN: Why specially Spain?

THE NEIGHBOUR: You hear such things about the stuff they're sending. A disgrace, I call it.

THE MAN: Best mind what you say.

THE NEIGHBOUR: You joined them now too?

THE MAN: I've not joined nothing. I get on with my work. Where's Martha gone?

THE NEIGHBOUR: I'd best warn you, I suppose. It could be something nasty. Just as I came in the postman was here, and there was some kind of letter got your wife all worked up. Made me wonder if I shouldn't ask the Schiermanns to lend me that bread.

THE MAN: Cor. *He calls:* Martha!

Enter his wife. She is in mourning.

THE MAN: What are you up to? Who's dead then?

THE WIFE: Franz. We got a letter.

She hands him a letter.

THE NEIGHBOUR: For God's sake! What happened to him?

THE MAN: It was an accident.

THE NEIGHBOUR *mistrustfully:* But wasn't he a pilot?

THE MAN: Yes.

THE NEIGHBOUR: And he had an accident?

THE MAN: At Stettin. In the course of a night exercise with troops, it says here.

THE NEIGHBOUR: He won't have had no accident. Tell me another.

THE MAN: I'm only telling you what it says here. The letter's from the commandant.

THE NEIGHBOUR: Did he write to you lately? From Stettin?

THE MAN: Don't get worked up, Martha. It won't help.

THE WIFE *sobbing:* No, I know.

THE NEIGHBOUR: He was such a nice fellow, that brother of yours. Like me to make you a pot of coffee?

THE MAN: Yes, if you would, Mrs Dietz.

THE NEIGHBOUR *looking for a pot:* That sort of thing's always a shock.

THE WIFE: Go on, have your wash, Herbert. Mrs Dietz won't mind.

THE MAN: There's no hurry.

THE NEIGHBOUR: So he wrote to you from Stettin?

THE MAN: That's where the letters always came from.

THE NEIGHBOUR *gives a look:* Really? I suppose he'd gone south with the others?

THE MAN: What do you mean, gone south?

THE NEIGHBOUR: Way south to sunny Spain.

THE MAN *as his wife again bursts into sobs:* Pull yourself together, Martha. You shouldn't say that sort of thing, Mrs Dietz.

THE NEIGHBOUR: I just wonder what they'd tell you in Stettin if you went and tried to collect your brother.

THE MAN: I'm not going to Stettin.

THE NEIGHBOUR: They always sweep things under the mat. They think it's heroic of them not to let anything come out. There was a fellow in the boozer bragging about how clever they are at covering up their war. When one of your bombers gets shot down and the blokes inside jump out with parachutes, the other bombers machine-gun them down in midair – their own blokes – so's they can't tell the Reds where they've come from.

THE WIFE *who is feeling sick:* Get us some water, will you, Herbert, I'm feeling sick.

THE NEIGHBOUR: I really didn't mean to upset you, it's just the way they cover it all up. They know it's criminal all right and that their war can't stand being exposed. Same in this case. Had an accident in the course of an exercise! What are they exercising at? A war, that's what!

THE MAN: Don't talk so loudly in here, d'you mind? *To his wife:* How are you feeling?

THE NEIGHBOUR: You're another of them keeps quiet
about it all. There's your answer, in that letter.

THE MAN: Just shut up, would you?

THE WIFE: Herbert!

THE NEIGHBOUR: So now it's 'shut up, would you?'. Because you got a job. Your brother-in-law got one too,
didn't he? Had an 'accident' with one of the same things
you're making in that factory.

THE MAN: I don't like that, Mrs Dietz. Me working on
'one of the same things'! What are all the rest of them
working on? What's your husband working on? Electric
bulbs, isn't it? I suppose they're not for war. Just to
give light. But what's the light for? To light tanks, eh?
Or a battleship? Or one of those same things? He's only
making light bulbs, though. My God, there's nothing
left that's not for war. How am I supposed to find a job
if I keep telling myself 'not for war!'? D'you want me
to starve?

THE NEIGHBOUR *subduedly:* I'm not saying you got to
starve. Of course you're right to take the job. I'm just
talking about those criminals. A nice kind of job creation,
I don't think.

THE MAN *seriously:* And better not go around in black like
that, Martha. They don't like it.

THE NEIGHBOUR: The questions it makes people ask:
that's what they don't like.

THE WIFE *calmly:* You'd rather I took it off?

THE MAN: Yes, if I'm not to lose my job any minute.

THE WIFE: I'm not taking it off.

THE MAN: What d'you mean?

THE WIFE: I'm not taking it off. My brother's dead. I'm
going into mourning.

THE MAN: If you hadn't got it because Rosa bought it when
Mother died, you wouldn't be able to go into mourning.

THE WIFE *shouting:* Don't anyone tell me I'm not going
into mourning! If they can slaughter him I have a right to
cry, don't I? I never heard of such a thing. It's the most
inhuman thing ever happened! They're criminals of the
lowest kind!

THE NEIGHBOUR *while the man sits speechless with horror:* But Mrs Fenn!

THE MAN *hoarsely:* If you're going to talk like that we could do more than lose our job.

THE WIFE: Let them come and get me, then! They've concentration camps for women too. Let them just put me in one of those because I dare to mind when they kill my brother! What was he in Spain for?

THE MAN: Shut up about Spain!

THE NEIGHBOUR: That kind of talk could get us into trouble, Mrs Fenn.

THE WIFE: Are we to keep quiet just because they might take your job away? Because we'll die of starvation if we don't make bombers for them? And die just the same if we do? Exactly like my Franz? They created a job for him too. Three foot under. He could as well have had that here.

THE MAN *holding a hand over her mouth:* Shut up, will you? It doesn't help.

THE WIFE: What does help then? Do something that does!

24

Consulting the People

> And as the column passes
> We call with urgent voices:
> Can none of you say No?
> You've got to make them heed you.
> This war to which they lead you
> Will soon be your death-blow.

Berlin. March 13th, 1938. A working-class flat, with two men and a woman. The constricted space is blocked by a flagpole. A great noise of jubilation from the radio, with church bells and the sound of aircraft. A voice is saying 'And now the Führer is about to enter Vienna.'

THE WOMAN: It's like the sea.

THE OLDER WORKER: Aye, it's one victory after another for that fellow.

THE YOUNGER WORKER: And us that gets defeated.

THE WOMAN: That's right.

THE YOUNGER WORKER: Listen to them shouting. Like they're being given a present.

THE OLDER WORKER: They are. An invasion.

THE YOUNGER WORKER: And then it's what they call 'consulting the People'. 'Ein Volk, ein Reich, ein Führer!' 'A single people, a single empire, a single leader.' 'Willst du das, Deutscher?' 'You're German, are you in favour?' And us not able to put out the least little leaflet about this referendum. Here, in a working-class district like Neukölln.

THE WOMAN: How d'you mean, not able?

THE YOUNGER WORKER: Too dangerous.

THE OLDER WORKER: And just when they've caught Karl. How are we to get the addresses?

THE YOUNGER WORKER: We'd need someone to do the writing too.

THE WOMAN *points at the radio:* He had a hundred thousand men to launch his attack. We need one man. Fine. If he's the only one who's got what's needed, then he'll score the victories.

THE YOUNGER WORKER *in anger:* So we can do without Karl.

THE WOMAN: If that's the way you people feel then we may as well split up.

THE OLDER WORKER: Comrades, there's no use kidding ourselves. Producing a leaflet's getting harder and harder, that's a fact. It's no good acting as if we just can't hear all that victory din – *pointing at the radio. To the woman:* You've got to admit, anyone hearing that sort of thing might think they're getting stronger all the time. It really does sound like a single people, wouldn't you say?

THE WOMAN: It sounds like twenty thousand drunks being stood free beer.

THE YOUNGER WORKER: For all you know we might be the only people to say so.

THE WOMAN: Right. Us and others like us.

The woman smoothes out a small crumpled piece of paper.

THE OLDER WORKER: What have you got there?

THE WOMAN: It's a copy of a letter. There's such a din I
can read it out. *She reads:*

'DEAR SON: TOMORROW I SHALL HAVE CEASED TO BE. EXECU-
TIONS ARE USUALLY AT SIX A.M. I'M WRITING NOW BECAUSE I
WANT YOU TO KNOW I HAVEN'T CHANGED MY OPINIONS, NOR
HAVE I APPLIED FOR A PARDON BECAUSE I DIDN'T COMMIT ANY
CRIME. I JUST SERVED MY COUNTRY. AND IF IT LOOKS AS
THOUGH I GOT NOWHERE LIKE THAT IT ISN'T SO. EVERY MAN TO
HIS POST, SHOULD BE OUR MOTTO. OUR TASK IS VERY DIFFICULT,
BUT IT'S THE GREATEST ONE THERE IS — TO FREE THE HUMAN
RACE FROM ITS OPPRESSORS. TILL THAT'S DONE LIFE HAS NO
OTHER VALUE. LET THAT OUT OF OUR SIGHTS AND THE WHOLE
HUMAN RACE WILL RELAPSE INTO BARBARISM. YOU'RE STILL
QUITE YOUNG BUT IT WON'T HURT YOU TO REMEMBER ALWAYS
WHICH SIDE YOU ARE ON. STICK WITH YOUR OWN CLASS, THEN
YOUR FATHER WON'T HAVE SUFFERED HIS UNHAPPY FATE IN
VAIN, BECAUSE IT ISN'T EASY. LOOK AFTER YOUR MOTHER,
YOUR BROTHERS AND SISTERS TOO, YOU'RE THE ELDEST. BETTER
BE CLEVER. GREETINGS TO YOU ALL YOUR LOVING FATHER.'

THE OLDER WORKER: There aren't really that few of us
after all.

THE YOUNGER WORKER: What's to go in the referendum
leaflet, then?

THE WOMAN *thinking:* Best thing would be just one word:
NO!

Señora Carrar's Rifles
partly based on an idea of J. M. Synge

Collaborator: M. STEFFIN

Translator: WOLFGANG SAUERLANDER

Characters
TERESA CARRAR, *a fisherwoman*
JOSÉ, *her younger son*
PEDRO JAQUERAS, *a worker, brother of Teresa Carrar*
THE WOUNDED MAN
MANUELA
THE PRIEST
OLD MRS PÉREZ
Two Fisherman
Women
Children

A fisherman's cottage in Andalusia on a night in April, 1937. In one corner of the whitewashed room a large black crucifix. Teresa Carrar, a fisherwoman of forty, is baking bread. Her son José, fifteen, stands at the open window, whittling a float. Roar of cannon in the distance.

THE MOTHER: Can you still see Juan's boat?

JOSÉ: Yes.

THE MOTHER: Is his lantern still burning?

JOSÉ: Yes.

THE MOTHER: No other boat joined him?

JOSÉ: No.

Pause.

THE MOTHER: That's strange. Why isn't anybody else out?

JOSÉ: You know why.

THE MOTHER *patiently:* If I knew, I wouldn't be asking.

JOSÉ: There's no one out but Juan; they've other things to do than catch fish these days.

THE MOTHER: I see.

Pause.

JOSÉ: If it was up to him Juan wouldn't be out either.

THE MOTHER: Right. It isn't up to him.

JOSÉ *whittling furiously:* No.

The mother puts the dough in the oven, wipes her hands and takes up a fish net to mend it.

JOSÉ: I'm hungry.

THE MOTHER: But you don't want your brother to go fishing.

JOSÉ: Because I can do that just as well and Juan ought to be at the front.

THE MOTHER: I thought you wanted to go to the front too.

Pause.

JOSÉ: Think the food ships will get through the British blockade?

THE MOTHER: Anyhow there'll be no flour left when this bread is done.

José shuts the window.

THE MOTHER: Why are you shutting the window?

JOSÉ: It's nine o'clock.

THE MOTHER: Well?

JOSÉ: That swine is on the radio at nine and the Pérezes will tune in.

THE MOTHER *imploringly:* Please open the window! You can't see properly with the light on in here and the window reflecting it.

JOSÉ: Why should I sit here and watch? He won't run away. You're just afraid he'll go to the front.

THE MOTHER: Don't answer back! It's bad enough my having to keep an eye on the two of you.

JOSÉ: What do you mean, the two of us?

THE MOTHER: You're no better than your brother. Worse if anything.

JOSÉ: They only put on the radio for our benefit. This'll be the third time. They opened their window on purpose yesterday to make us listen; I saw them.

THE MOTHER: Those speeches are no different from the ones they make in Valencia.

JOSÉ: Why not just say they're better?

THE MOTHER: You know I don't think they're better. Why should I be for the generals? I'm against bloodshed.

JOSÉ: Who started it? Us, I suppose?

The mother is silent. José has opened the window again. An announcement is heard from a near-by radio: 'Attention; Attention! His Excellency General Queipo de Llano will address you.' The radio general's voice comes through the night loud and clear as he delivers his nightly address to the Spanish people.

THE GENERAL'S VOICE: Today or tomorrow, my friends, we propose to have a serious word with you. And we propose to have that word with you in Madrid, even if what's left of it doesn't look like Madrid any more. Then the Archbishop of Canterbury will really have something to shed crocodile tears for. Just wait till our splendid Moors are through.

JOSÉ: Bastard!

THE GENERAL'S VOICE: My friends, the so-called British

Empire, that colossus on feet of clay, cannot stop us destroying the capital of a perverted people that has the effrontery to oppose the irresistible cause of nationalism. Rabble! We'll wipe them off the face of the earth!

JOSÉ: That's us, mother.

THE MOTHER: We're not rebels and we're not opposing anybody. Perhaps you boys would if you had your way. You and that brother of yours, you're both reckless. You got that from your father and maybe I wouldn't like it if you were different. But this thing is no joke. Can't you hear their guns? We're poor; poor people can't make war. *Knocking at the door. Pedro Jaqueras, a worker, Teresa Carrar's brother, enters. It is plain that he has walked a long way.*

THE WORKER: Good evening.

JOSÉ: Uncle Pedro!

THE MOTHER: What brings you here, Pedro? *She shakes hands with him.*

JOSÉ: Have you come from Motril, Uncle Pedro? How are things going?

THE WORKER: Ah, not too well. How are you getting along here?

THE MOTHER *hesitantly:* Not too bad.

JOSÉ: Did you leave today?

THE WORKER: Yes.

JOSÉ: Takes a good four hours, eh?

THE WORKER: More; the roads are clogged with refugees trying to get to Almería.

JOSÉ: But Motril's holding out?

THE WORKER: I don't know what has happened today. Last night we were still holding out.

JOSÉ: Then why did you leave?

THE WORKER: We need some stuff for the front. So I figured I'd look in on you.

THE MOTHER: Would you like a sip of wine? *She fetches wine.* The bread won't be done for another half hour.

THE WORKER: Where's Juan?

JOSÉ: Out fishing.

THE WORKER: Fishing?

JOSÉ: You can see his lantern from the window.

THE MOTHER: We've got to live.

THE WORKER: Of course. As I was coming down the street I heard the radio general. Who listens to him around here?

JOSÉ: The Pérezes across the street.

THE WORKER: Do they always tune in on that stuff?

JOSÉ: No. They're not Franco people, it isn't for their own benefit, if that's what you mean.

THE WORKER: Is that so?

THE MOTHER *to José:* Are you keeping an eye on your brother?

JOSÉ *reluctantly returns to the window:* Don't worry, he hasn't fallen overboard.

The worker takes the wine jug, sits down by his sister and helps her mend the nets.

THE WORKER: How old would Juan be now?

THE MOTHER: Twenty-one in September.

THE WORKER: And José?

THE MOTHER: Have you got something special to do around here?

THE WORKER: Nothing special.

THE MOTHER: You haven't shown your face in a long time.

THE WORKER: Two years.

THE MOTHER: How's Rosa?

THE WORKER: Rheumatism.

THE MOTHER: The two of you might have dropped in once in a while.

THE WORKER: I guess Rosa was a little put out about Carlos's funeral.

The mother is silent.

THE WORKER: She said you might have let us know. Of course we'd have come to your husband's funeral, Teresa.

THE MOTHER: It was all so sudden.

THE WORKER: What actually happened?

The mother is silent.

JOSÉ: Shot through the lung.

THE WORKER *amazed:* How come?

THE MOTHER: What do you mean 'How come'?

THE WORKER: Everything was quiet around here two years ago.

JOSÉ: There was the rising in Oviedo.

THE WORKER: How did Carlos get to Oviedo?

THE MOTHER: Took the train.

THE WORKER: From here?

JOSÉ: Yes, when he read about the rising in the papers.

THE MOTHER *with bitterness:* Same as other people go to America to stake everything on one card. Fools.

JOSÉ *rising:* Are you saying he was a fool?

Silently, with trembling hands, she lays the net aside and goes out.

THE WORKER: Must have been pretty bad for her.

JOSÉ: Yes.

THE WORKER: Did she take it very hard when he didn't come back?

JOSÉ: He did come back, she saw him again. That was the worst part of it. Up there in the Asturias, he seems to have managed to take a train with a field dressing under his blouse. He had to change twice, and then he died here at the station. One evening our door suddenly opened and the local women filed in, the way they do when someone gets drowned. They lined up along the walls without a word and reeled off an Ave Maria. Then he was brought in on a piece of sailcloth and laid down on the floor. She's been scurrying off to church ever since. And refusing to see the school teacher that everybody knew was a red.

THE WORKER: You mean she's got religion?

JOSÉ *nods:* Juan thinks it was mostly because people round here started talking about her.

THE WORKER: What did they say?

JOSÉ: That she put him up to it.

THE WORKER: Well, did she?

José shrugs his shoulders. The mother returns, looks into the oven and sits down again with the net.

THE MOTHER *to the worker who is again trying to help her:* Never mind that. Drink your wine and take it easy, you've been up and about since early morning.

The worker takes the wine jug and returns to the table.

THE MOTHER: Do you want to stay the night?

THE WORKER: No. I haven't that much time. I've got to
   go back tonight. But I'd like to wash. *He goes out.*

THE MOTHER *beckons José to come to her:* Did he tell you
   what he came for?

JOSÉ: No.

THE MOTHER: Are you sure?
   The worker returns with a wash basin; he washes himself.

THE MOTHER: Are the old Lópezes still alive?

THE WORKER: Only him. *To José:* I suppose a good many
   of the villagers have gone to the front?

JOSÉ: Some are still here.

THE WORKER: In our town a lot of good Catholics have
   joined up.

JOSÉ: Some from here too.

THE WORKER: Have they all got rifles?

JOSÉ: No. Not all.

THE WORKER: That's bad. Guns are the main thing now.
   Aren't there any rifles left in this village?

THE MOTHER *quickly:* No!

JOSÉ: Some people hide them. They bury them like
   potatoes.
   The Mother looks at José.

THE WORKER: I see.
   *José ambles away from the window and withdraws into the back-
   ground.*

THE MOTHER: Where are you going?

JOSÉ: Nowhere.

THE MOTHER: Get back to that window!
   José remains obstinately in the rear.

THE WORKER: What's going on here?

THE MOTHER: Why have you left the window? Answer me!

THE WORKER: Is there someone outside?

JOSÉ *hoarsely:* No.
   Children's voices are heard howling outside.

CHILDREN'S VOICES:
   Juan's not a soldier
   He'd rather stay in bed.
   Juan's a lousy coward
   Pulls the blanket over his head.

Three children's faces appear in the window.

THE CHILDREN: Baah! *They run away.*

THE MOTHER *gets up, goes to the window:* Just let me catch you and I'll beat the stuffing out of you, stinking brats! *Talking back into the room.* It's those Pérezes again!
Pause.

THE WORKER: You used to play cards, José. How about a little game?
The mother sits down at the window. José gets the cards and they start playing.

THE WORKER: Do you still cheat?

JOSÉ *laughing:* Did I?

THE WORKER: Used to think so. I'll just cut to be on the safe side. Right then, anything goes. All's fair in cards and war.
The Mother looks up suspiciously.

JOSÉ: What lousy trumps.

THE WORKER: Thanks for letting me know. – Ha, look at him playing the ace of trumps. That was a bluff, but it didn't pay off, did it? Fired your big gun, and now here I come with my peashooter. *Slaps him down with a series of quick tricks.* You had it coming. Daring is all very well, my boy. You're daring all right, but you've a lot to learn about caution.

JOSÉ: Nothing venture, nothing gain.

THE MOTHER: They got those sayings from their father. 'A gentleman takes risks.' That it?

THE WORKER: Yes, he risks our skins. Don Miguel de Ferrante once lost seventy peasants to a colonel in a single card game. He was ruined, poor devil; had to make do with twelve servants for the rest of his life. – Look at that, he's playing his last ten.

JOSÉ: I had to. *He takes the trick.* It was my only chance.

THE MOTHER: That's the way they are. His father used to jump out of the boat when his net got caught.

THE WORKER: Maybe he didn't have all that many nets.

THE MOTHER: Didn't have all that many lives either.
In the doorway stands a man in the uniform of the militia. His head is bandaged, one arm is in a sling.

THE MOTHER: Come on in, Pablo.

THE WOUNDED MAN: You said I could come back to be bandaged, Mrs Carrar.

THE MOTHER: It's all soaked through again. *She runs out.*

THE WORKER: Where'd you get that?

THE WOUNDED MAN: Monte Solluve.

The mother returns with a shirt which she tears into strips. She renews the dressing, constantly keeping an eye on those at the table.

THE MOTHER: You've been working again, then.

THE WOUNDED MAN: Only with my right arm.

THE MOTHER: But they told you not to.

THE WOUNDED MAN: Yes, I know. – The rumour is, they'll break through tonight. We've no reserves left. Could they be through already?

THE WORKER *getting restless:* No, I don't think so. The gunfire would sound different.

THE WOUNDED MAN: That's right.

THE MOTHER: Am I hurting you? You must tell me. I'm not a trained nurse. I'm doing it as gently as I can.

JOSÉ: They'll never break through at Madrid.

THE WOUNDED MAN: There's no telling.

JOSÉ: Oh yes there is.

THE WOUNDED MAN: Fine. But you've gone and torn up another good shirt, Mrs Carrar. You shouldn't have done that.

THE MOTHER: Would you sooner have a dishrag around your arm?

THE WOUNDED MAN: You people aren't so well off either.

THE MOTHER: While it lasts it lasts. There now. But there wouldn't be enough for your other arm.

THE WOUNDED MAN *laughs:* I'll have to be more careful next time. *Gets up; to the worker:* If only they don't break through, the bastards! *He leaves.*

THE MOTHER: Oh God, those guns!

JOSÉ: And we go fishing.

THE MOTHER: You two can be glad you've still got sound limbs.

The swelling and fading noise of trucks and singing is heard from outside. The worker and José step to the window and watch.

THE WORKER: That's the International Brigade. They're being sent to the Motril front.

The refrain of the 'Thälmann Column' is heard: 'Die Heimat ist weit . . .'.

THE WORKER: Those are the Germans.

A few measures of the Marseillaise.

THE WORKER: The French.

The Warszawianka.

THE WORKER: Poles.

Bandiera rossa.

THE WORKER: The Italians.

Hold the Fort.

THE WORKER: Americans.

Los cuatro generales.

THE WORKER: And that's our men.

The noise of trucks and singing fades away. The worker and José return to the table.

THE WORKER: Everything depends on tonight! – I really ought to be going. That was the last hand, José.

THE MOTHER *approaching the table:* Who won?

JOSÉ *proudly:* He did.

THE MOTHER: Shouldn't I make up a bed for you?

THE WORKER: No, I've got to be going. *But he remains seated.*

THE MOTHER: Give Rosa my regards. And tell her to let bygones be bygones. None of us knows what's going to happen.

JOSÉ: I'll go a bit of the way with you.

THE WORKER: No need.

The mother, standing up, looks out of the window.

THE MOTHER: I suppose you'd have liked to see Juan?

THE WORKER: Yes, I'd have liked to. But he won't be back all that soon, will he?

THE MOTHER: He's gone pretty far out. Must be close to the Cape. *Talking back into the room.* We could go and get him.

A young girl appears in the doorway.

JOSÉ: Hello, Manuela. *Under his breath to the worker:* It's Juan's girl, Manuela. *To the young girl:* This is Uncle Pedro.

THE YOUNG GIRL: Where's Juan?

THE MOTHER: Juan's at work.

THE YOUNG GIRL: We thought you'd bundled him off to kindergarten to play ball.

THE MOTHER: No, he went fishing. Juan's a fisherman.

THE YOUNG GIRL: Why didn't he come to the meeting at the schoolhouse? Some of the fishermen were there.

THE MOTHER: He had no business there.

JOSÉ: What was the meeting about?

THE YOUNG GIRL: They decided whoever can be spared must go to the front this very night. You people knew what the meeting was about. We sent Juan a message.

JOSÉ: That's not possible. Juan wouldn't have gone fishing in that case. Or did they tell you, Mother?

The mother is silent. She has crawled all the way into the oven.

JOSÉ: She didn't give him the message! *To the mother:* So that's why you sent him out fishing!

THE WORKER: You shouldn't have done that, Teresa!

THE MOTHER *straightening up:* God gave people trades. My son is a fisherman.

THE YOUNG GIRL: Do you want to make us the laughing stock of the whole village? Wherever I go people point at me. Just hearing Juan's name makes me sick. What kind of people are you anyway?

THE MOTHER: We're poor people.

THE YOUNG GIRL: The government has called on all able-bodied men to take up arms. Don't tell me you didn't read that.

THE MOTHER: I've read it. Government this, government that. I know they want us to end up in the boneyard. But I'm not volunteering to wheel my children there.

THE YOUNG GIRL: No. Sooner wait till they're lined up against the wall, wouldn't you? I've never seen anything so stupid. It's because of your sort that things are how they are and a swine like Queipo dares talk to us the way he does.

THE MOTHER *weakly:* I'm not having such things said in my house.

THE YOUNG GIRL *beside herself:* She's all for the generals now, I suppose.

JOSÉ *somewhat impatiently:* No! But she doesn't want us to fight.

THE WORKER: Neutrality: that it?

THE MOTHER: I know you people want to turn my house into a den of conspirators. And *you* won't lay off till you see Juan stood up against a wall.

THE YOUNG GIRL: And they said *you* helped your husband when he went off to Oviedo.

THE MOTHER *softly:* Hold your tongue! I did not help my husband. Not for a thing like that. I know I'm being blamed for it, but it's a lie. All dirty lies! Anybody'll tell you.

THE YOUNG GIRL: Nobody's blaming you, Mrs Carrar. They said that with the deepest respect. All of us in the village knew that Carlos Carrar was a hero. But now we know that he probably had to sneak out of the house in the dead of night.

JOSÉ: My father did not sneak out of the house in the dead of night, Manuela.

THE MOTHER: Shut up, José!

THE YOUNG GIRL: Tell your son I'm through with him. And there'll be no more need for him to keep out of sight for fear I'll ask why he isn't where he should be. *She leaves.*

THE WORKER: You oughtn't to have let the girl go like that, Teresa. In the old days you wouldn't have.

THE MOTHER: I'm the same as I've always been. They probably made bets to see who could get Juan off to the front. – Anyway, I'll go and get him. Or you go, José. No, wait, better go myself. I'll be right back. *Goes out.*

THE WORKER: Look, José, you're not stupid, there's no need to tell you a story you know already. All right, where are they?

JOSÉ: What?

THE WORKER: The rifles.

JOSÉ: Father's?

THE WORKER: They must be around somewhere. He couldn't have taken them on the train when he went off.

JOSÉ: That what you came for?

THE WORKER: What else?

JOSÉ: She'll never let them go. She's hidden them.

THE WORKER: Where?

José indicates a corner. The worker gets up and is starting in that direction when they hear footsteps.

THE WORKER *sits down quickly.* Quiet now!

The mother comes in with the local priest. He is a tall, strong man in a worn-out cassock.

THE PRIEST: Good evening, José. *To the worker:* Good evening.

THE MOTHER: Father, this is my brother from Motril.

THE PRIEST: I'm glad to make your acquaintance. *To the mother:* I really must apologise for coming with yet another request. Could you stop in at the Turillos' at noon tomorrow? Mrs Turillo has joined her husband at the front and now the children are alone.

THE MOTHER: I'll be glad to.

THE PRIEST *to the worker:* What brings you to our village? I'm told it's not so easy to get here from Motril.

THE WORKER: Still pretty quiet around here, ain't it?

THE PRIEST: Beg your pardon? – Yes.

THE MOTHER: Pedro, I believe the Father asked you something. What brings you here?

THE WORKER: I figured it was time to see how my sister was getting along.

THE PRIEST *with an encouraging glance at the mother:* It's very kind of you to take an interest in your sister. As you probably know, she's been having a hard time of it.

THE WORKER: I hope you find her a good parishioner.

THE MOTHER: You must take a sip of wine. – The Father keeps an eye on children whose parents have gone to the front. You've been running around all day again, haven't you? *She puts down a jug of wine for the priest.*

THE PRIEST *sits down, takes the jug:* If only I know who was going to get me a new pair of shoes.

At this moment the Pérezes' radio starts up again. The mother is about to close the window.

THE PRIEST: You can have the window open, Mrs Carrar. They saw me come in. They resent my not mounting the barricades, so they treat me to one of those speeches now and then.

THE WORKER: Does it bother you much?

THE PRIEST: As a matter of fact, it does. But never mind, leave the window open.

THE GENERAL'S VOICE: ... but we know the dastardly lies with which they try to besmirch the national cause. We may not pay the Archbishop of Canterbury as much as the Reds do, but to make up for that we could give him the names of ten thousand dead priests, whose throats have been cut by his honourable friends. Even if there's no cheque with the message, there is one thing his Grace ought to know: in the course of its victorious advance, the nationalist army has found plenty of hidden bombs and arms, but not one surviving priest.

The worker offers the priest his pack of cigarettes. The priest takes one with a smile, though he is no smoker.

THE GENERAL'S VOICE: Fortunately, the right cause can win without depending on Archbishops so long as it has decent planes. And men like General Franco, General Mola ... *The broadcast is abruptly cut off.*

THE PRIEST *good-humouredly:* Thank God, even the Pérezes can't stand more than three sentences of that stuff! I can't believe speeches like that make a good impression.

THE WORKER: They say even the Vatican is putting out the same kind of lies.

THE PRIEST: I don't know. *Miserably.* In my opinion it's not the Church's job to turn black into white and vice versa.

THE WORKER, *looking at José:* Certainly not.

THE MOTHER, *hastily:* My brother's with the militia, Father.

THE PRIEST: In which sector?

THE WORKER: Málaga.

THE PRIEST: It must be horrible.

The worker smokes in silence.

THE MOTHER: My brother thinks I'm not a good Spaniard. He says I ought to let Juan go to the front.

JOSÉ: And me too. That's where we belong.

THE PRIEST: You know, of course, Señora Carrar, that in my heart and conscience I consider your attitude justified. In many places the lower clergy are supporting the legal government. Out of eighteen parishes in Bilbao seventeen have declared for the government. Quite a few of my fellow priests are doing service at the front. Some have been killed. But I myself am not a fighter. God has not given me the gift of marshalling my parishioners in a loud clear voice to fight for – *groping for a word* – anything. I stand by the Lord's commandment: 'Thou shalt not kill.' I am not a rich man. I don't own a monastery and what little I have I share with my flock. Maybe that is what gives my words a certain weight in times like these.

THE WORKER: True. But maybe you're more of a fighter than you think. Please don't misunderstand me. But suppose a man is about to be killed and wants to defend himself; then you tie his hands with your 'Thou shalt not kill', so he lets himself be slaughtered like an ox; in that case, perhaps, you'd be participating in the fight – in your own way of course? If you'll forgive me for saying so.

THE PRIEST: For the time being I'm participating in hunger.

THE WORKER: And how do you think we'll get back the daily bread you ask for in the Lord's Prayer?

THE PRIEST: I don't know. I can only pray.

THE WORKER: Then you might be interested to know that God made the supply ships turn back last night.

JOSÉ: Is that true? – Mother, the ships have turned back.

THE WORKER: Yes, that's neutrality. *Suddenly.* You're neutral too, aren't you?

THE PRIEST: What do you mean by that?

THE WORKER: Let's say, in favour of non-intervention. And by being for non-intervention you objectively approve every bloodbath the generals inflict on the Spanish people.

THE PRIEST *raising his hands level with his head in protest:* I don't approve at all.

THE WORKER *looks at him with half-closed eyes:* Keep your

hands like that for a moment. With that gesture, I've heard, five thousand of our people stepped out of their besieged houses in Badajoz. With that gesture they were gunned down.

THE MOTHER: Pedro, how can you say such a thing!

THE WORKER: It only struck me, Teresa, that the gesture of disapproval is horribly like the gesture of capitulation. I've often read that people who wash their hands in innocence do so in blood-stained basins. And their hands bear the traces.

THE MOTHER: Pedro!

THE PRIEST: Never mind, Mrs Carrar. Tempers are heated at a time like this. We shall take a calmer attitude when it's all over.

THE WORKER: I thought we were to be wiped off the face of the earth because we are a perverted people.

THE PRIEST: Who says such things?

THE WORKER: The radio general. Didn't you hear him just now? You don't listen to the radio enough.

THE PRIEST *disgustedly:* Oh, that general . . .

THE WORKER: Don't say 'Oh, that general'! That general has hired all the scum of Spain to wipe us off the face of the earth, not to mention the Moors, Italians and Germans.

THE MOTHER: Yes, they shouldn't have brought in all those people who just do it for money.

THE PRIEST: Don't you think there might be some sincere people on the other side too?

THE WORKER: I don't see what they could be sincere about.

Pause.

THE PRIEST *takes out his watch:* I've still got to call on the Turillos.

THE WORKER: The government had a clear majority in the Chamber of Deputies. Don't you believe the election was honest and above-board?

THE PRIEST: Yes, I do.

THE WORKER: When I spoke about tying the hands of a man who wants to defend himself, I meant it literally, because we haven't got all that much apart from our bare hands and . . .

THE MOTHER *interrupting him:* Please, don't start in again, it's no use.

THE PRIEST: Man is born with bare hands, as we all know. The Creator does not bring him forth from the womb with a weapon in his hand. I know the theory that all the misery in the world comes from the fact that the fisherman and the worker – you are a worker, I believe – have only their bare hands to fight for their livelihood with. But nowhere does Scripture say that this is a perfect world. On the contrary, it is full of misery, sin and oppression. Blessed the man who perchance may suffer from being sent into this world unarmed, but can at least leave it without a weapon in his hand.

THE WORKER: You said that beautifully. I won't contradict anything that sounds so beautiful. I only wish it impressed General Franco. The trouble is that General Franco is armed to the teeth and hasn't shown the slightest inclination to depart from this world. We'd gladly throw all the weapons in Spain after him if only he'd leave this world. Here's a leaflet his pilots have thrown down to us. I picked it up on the street in Motril. *He takes a leaflet from his pocket. The padre, the mother and José look at it.*

JOSÉ *to the mother:* You see? It's always the same, they're going to destroy everything.

THE MOTHER *while reading:* They can't do that.

THE WORKER: Oh yes, they can. What do you think, Father?

JOSÉ: Yes!

THE PRIEST, *not sure:* Well, technically, I think, they might be able to. But if I understand Mrs Carrar correctly, she means that it's not just a question of aeroplanes. They may be making these threats in their leaflets in order to convince the population of the seriousness of the situation; but to carry out such threats for military reasons would be a very different matter.

THE WORKER: I don't quite follow you.

JOSÉ: Neither do I.

THE PRIEST, *even less sure:* I thought I was being very clear.

THE WORKER: Your sentences are clear, but your opinion is not clear to me or José. You mean they're not going to drop bombs?

A short pause.

THE PRIEST: I believe it's a threat.

THE WORKER: Which won't be carried out?

THE PRIEST: No.

THE MOTHER: The way I see it, they're trying to avoid bloodshed by warning us not to resist them.

JOSÉ: Generals avoiding bloodshed?

THE MOTHER *showing him the leaflet:* Here it says: All who lay down their arms will be spared.

THE WORKER: In that case, I have another question for you, Father: Do you believe the people who lay down their arms will be spared?

THE PRIEST *looking around helplessly:* They say General Franco himself always makes it very clear that he is a Christian.

THE WORKER: Meaning he'll keep his promise?

THE PRIEST *vehemently:* He must keep it, Mr Jaqueras!

THE MOTHER: They can't do anything to the people who don't bear arms.

THE WORKER: Look, Father – *apologetic* – I don't know your name . . .

THE PRIEST: Francisco.

THE WORKER *continuing:* . . . Francisco, I didn't mean to ask you what in your opinion General Franco *must* do but what in your opinion he *will* do. You understand my question?

THE PRIEST: Yes.

THE WORKER: You understand that I'm asking you as a Christian, or maybe we should say, as a man who doesn't own a monastery, to use your own words, and who will tell the truth when it's a matter of life and death. Because it is, don't you agree?

THE PRIEST, *very upset:* I understand.

THE WORKER: It might make it easier for you to answer if I remind you of what happened in Málaga.

THE PRIEST: I know what you mean. But are you sure there was no resistance in Málaga?

THE WORKER: You know that fifty thousand men, women and children were mowed down by shelling from Franco's ships and by bombs and machinegun fire from his planes, while trying to escape to Almería on a highway that's a hundred and forty miles long.

THE PRIEST: That might be an atrocity story.

THE WORKER: Like the one about the executed priests?

THE PRIEST: Like the one about the executed priests.

THE WORKER: In other words they weren't mowed down?
The priest is silent.

THE WORKER: Mrs Carrar and her sons are not taking up arms against General Franco. Does that mean Mrs Carrar and her sons are safe?

THE PRIEST: To the best of my knowledge . . .

THE WORKER: Really? To the best of your knowledge?

THE PRIEST *in agitation:* Surely you don't want me to give you a guarantee?

THE WORKER: No. I only want you to give me your true opinion. Are Mrs Carrar and her sons safe?
The priest is silent.

THE WORKER: I think we understand your answer. You're an honest man.

THE PRIEST *getting up, confused:* Well, Mrs Carrar, then I can count on you to look after the Turillo children?

THE MOTHER *also quite disconcerted:* I'll take them something to eat. And thank you for your visit.
The priest nods to the worker and José as he leaves. The mother accompanies him.

JOSÉ: Now you've heard the kind of stuff they're drumming into her. But don't leave without the rifles.

THE WORKER: Where are they? Quick!
They go to the rear, remove a chest and rip the floor open.

JOSÉ: She'll be back in a second.

THE WORKER: We'll put the rifles outside the window. I can pick them up later.
Hurriedly they take the rifles from a wooden box. A small tattered flag in which they were wrapped falls to the floor.

JOSÉ: And there's the little flag from the old days. How could you sit still so long when it's so urgent?

THE WORKER: I had to have them.

Both are testing the rifles. José suddenly pulls a cap – the cap of the militia – from his pocket and puts it on triumphantly.

THE WORKER: Where the hell did you get that?

JOSÉ: Swapped it. *With a furtive glance at the door he puts it back in his pocket.*

THE MOTHER *has come in again:* Put those rifles back! Is that what you came for?

THE WORKER: Yes, we need them, Teresa. We can't stop the generals with our bare hands.

JOSÉ: Now you've heard from Father Francisco himself how things really are.

THE MOTHER: If you came just to get the rifles you needn't wait any longer. And if you people don't leave us in peace, I'll take my children and clear out.

THE WORKER: Teresa, have you ever looked at our country on a map? We're living on a broken platter. Where the break is there's water, around the edge there are guns. And above us are the bombers. Where will you go? Straight into the guns?

She goes up to him, takes the rifles from his hands and carries them off in her arms.

THE MOTHER: Your lot can't have the rifles, Pedro.

JOSÉ: You've got to let him have them, Mother. Here they'll only rot away.

THE MOTHER: You shut up, José! What do you know about these things?

THE WORKER *has calmly sat down on his chair again and lights a cigarette:* Teresa, you have no right to hold back Carlos's rifles.

THE MOTHER *packing the rifles in the box:* Right or no right: you can't have them. You can't just rip up my floor and take things out of my house against my will.

THE WORKER: These things aren't exactly part of the house. I won't tell you what I think of you in front of your boy and we won't argue about what your husband would think of you. He fought. I suppose it's worry about your boys that's affected your mind. But of course we can't let that influence us.

THE MOTHER: What do you mean?

THE WORKER: I mean that I'm not leaving without the rifles. That's definite.

THE MOTHER: You'll have to knock me down first.

THE WORKER: That I won't do. I'm not General Franco. But I'll talk to Juan. That way I'll get them.

THE MOTHER, *quickly:* Juan won't be back.

JOSÉ: But you called him yourself!

THE MOTHER: I did not call him. I don't want him to see you, Pedro.

THE WORKER: I thought as much. But I have a voice too. I can go down to the shore and call him. Two, three words will do it, Teresa, I know Juan. He's no coward. You can't hold him back.

JOSÉ: I'll go with you.

THE MOTHER, *very calmly:* Leave my children alone, Pedro. I told them I'd hang myself if they went. I know it's a great sin before God and gets you eternal damnation. But there's nothing else for me to do. When Carlos died – died the way he did – I went to see Father Francisco or I'd have hanged myself then. I know perfectly well that I was partly to blame, though he was the worst of the lot with his hot temper and his violent ways. We aren't all that well off, and it isn't an easy life to bear. But guns won't help. I realised that when they brought him in and laid him out on the floor. I'm not for the generals and it's disgraceful to say I am. But if I keep quiet and watch my temper, maybe they'll leave us in peace. It's a very simple calculation. I'm not asking much. I don't want to see this flag any more. We're unhappy enough as it is.

She calmly walks over to the little flag, picks it up and rips it apart. At once she stoops down, collects the tatters and puts them in her pocket.

THE WORKER: It would be better if you hanged yourself, Teresa.

Knocking at the door. Mrs Pérez, an old woman in black, comes in.

JOSÉ, *to the worker:* That's old Mrs Pérez.

THE WORKER *under his breath:* What kind of people are they?

JOSÉ: Good people. The ones with the radio. Her daughter was killed at the front last week.

OLD MRS PÉREZ: I waited until I saw the Father leave. I thought I ought to drop in, on account of my family. I wanted to tell you I don't think it's right of them to make trouble for you because of your opinions.

The mother is silent.

OLD MRS PÉREZ, *who has sat down:* You're worried about your children, Mrs Carrar. People always forget how hard it is to bring up children in times like these. I had seven. *She half turns to the worker to whom she has not been introduced.* There aren't many left now that Inez has been killed. I lost two before they were six. Those were the lean years of ninety-eight and ninety-nine. I don't even know where Andrés is. He last wrote from Rio. That's in South America. Mariana, as you know, is in Madrid. She has had a hard time too. She never was very strong. It always seems to us old people as if the younger folk had turned out kind of sickly.

THE MOTHER: But you still have Fernando.

OLD MRS PÉREZ: Yes.

THE MOTHER *confused:* I'm sorry, I didn't mean to offend you.

OLD MRS PÉREZ *calmly:* No need to apologise. I know you didn't.

JOSÉ *softly to the worker:* He's with Franco.

OLD MRS PÉREZ *quietly:* We don't talk about Fernando any more. *After a short pause.* You know, you can't really understand my family unless you keep in mind that we're all in great sorrow over Inez's death.

THE MOTHER: We were always very fond of Inez. *To the worker:* She taught Juan to read.

JOSÉ: Me too.

OLD MRS PÉREZ: Some people think you're for the other side. But I always contradict them. Our kind knows the difference between rich and poor.

THE MOTHER: I don't want my boys to be soldiers. They're not cattle to be slaughtered.

OLD MRS PÉREZ: You know, Mrs Carrar, I always say there's no life insurance for the poor. I mean they get it either way. The ones who get it all the time are the ones we call the poor people. No amount of foresight can save the poor, Mrs Carrar. Our Inez was always the most timid of the children. You can't imagine how my husband had to coax her before she got up the courage to swim.

THE MOTHER: What I mean is that she could still be living.

OLD MRS PÉREZ: But how would she be living?

THE MOTHER: Why did your daughter, a teacher, have to take up a gun and fight the generals?

THE WORKER: Who are being financed by the Holy Father, no less.

OLD MRS PÉREZ: She said she wanted to go on being a teacher.

THE MOTHER: Couldn't she have done just that at her school in Málaga, generals or no generals?

OLD MRS PÉREZ: We discussed that with her. Her father gave up smoking for seven years and her brothers and sisters never got a drop of milk in all that time so she could become a schoolteacher. But then Inez said she couldn't teach children that twice two is five and that General Franco was sent by God.

THE MOTHER: If Juan were to come and tell me he wouldn't be able to fish any more I'd let him have a piece of my mind. Do you think the speculators would give up trying to skin us if we got rid of the generals?

THE WORKER: I think it will be slightly harder for them when we have the guns.

THE MOTHER: Guns again, always guns! The shooting will never stop.

THE WORKER: That's not the point. If sharks attack you, are you the one that's using force? Did we march on Madrid or did General Mola come down over the mountains? For two years there was a little light, a very feeble light, not really a dawn, but now it's to be night again. And that's not the whole of it. It's not just that teachers won't be allowed to tell children that twice two is four, they're to be exterminated if they ever said so in the past. Didn't you hear him spell out tonight that we're to be wiped off the face of the earth?

THE MOTHER: Only those who have taken up arms. Don't hammer at me like this all the time. I can't argue with all of you. My sons look at me as if I were a policeman. When the flour chest is empty, I can see in their faces that I'm to blame. When the planes appear, they look away as if I had sent them. Why does Father Francisco keep silent when he ought to speak out? You all think I'm out of my mind because I believe the generals are human beings too, very wicked, yes, but not an earthquake you can't argue with. Why do you sit down in my room, Mrs Pérez, and keep telling me these things? Do you really think I don't know everything you're saying? Your daughter's been killed; now its to be the turn of my boys. Is that what you want? You haunt my house like bloody tax collectors, but I've already paid.

OLD MRS PÉREZ *getting up:* Mrs Carrar, I didn't mean to make you angry. I don't agree with my husband that you should be forced to do anything. We thought a lot of your husband, and I only wanted to apologise if my family is bothering you. *She leaves, nodding to the worker and José.*

Pause.

THE MOTHER: The worst of it is, the way they keep on at me they goad me into saying things I don't mean at all. I'm not against Inez.

THE WORKER *furious:* Yes, you are against Inez. By not helping her you were against her. You keep on saying you're not for the generals. And that's not true either, whether you know it or not. If you don't help us against them, you're for them. You can't stay neutral, Teresa.

JOSÉ *suddenly walking up to her:* Come on, mother, you haven't got a chance. *To the worker:* She's gone and sat on the box to keep us from getting them. Come on, mother, let's have them.

THE MOTHER: Best wipe the snot off your nose, José.

JOSÉ: Mother, I want to go with Uncle Pedro. I'm not

waiting here till they slaughter us like pigs. You can't stop me fighting like you stopped me smoking. There's Felipe who can't sling a stone half as straight as me, and he's at the front already, and Andrés is a year younger than me and he's been killed. I won't have the whole village laughing at me.

THE MOTHER: Yes, I know. Little Pablo promised a truck driver his dead mole if he'd take him to the front. That's ridiculous.

THE WORKER: It's not ridiculous.

JOSÉ: Tell Ernesto Turillo he can have my little boat. — Let's go, Uncle Pedro. *He intends to leave.*

THE MOTHER: You stay right here!

JOSÉ: No, I'm going. You can say you need Juan, but if he's here you don't need me too.

THE MOTHER: I'm not keeping Juan just to fish for me. And I won't let you go either. *She rushes to him and embraces him.* You can smoke if you like, and if you want to go fishing by yourself, I won't say a word, even in father's boat once in a while.

JOSÉ: Let go of me!

THE MOTHER: No, you're staying here.

JOSÉ *trying to free himself:* No, I'm going. — Quick, take the rifles, Uncle!

THE MOTHER: Oh!

She releases José and limps away, putting one foot down gingerly.

JOSÉ: What's wrong?

THE MOTHER: A fat lot you mind. Just go. You've got the better of your mother.

JOSÉ *suspiciously:* I wasn't rough. You can't be hurt.

THE MOTHER *massaging her foot:* Of course not. Run along.

THE WORKER: Want me to set it for you?

THE MOTHER: No, I want you to go. Out of my house! How dare you incite my children to assault me.

JOSÉ *furiously:* Me assault her! *White with rage he goes to the rear.*

THE MOTHER: You'll finish up a criminal. Why not take the last loaf of bread from the oven too? Yes, you could tie me to the chair with a rope. After all there are two of you.

THE WORKER: Stop playing games.

THE MOTHER: Juan is another madman, but he'd never use force against his mother. He'll give you what for when he gets back. Juan. *She suddenly gets up, struck by an idea, and rushes to the window. She forgets to limp and José indignantly points at her feet.*

JOSÉ: All of a sudden her foot's all right.

THE MOTHER *looks out; suddenly:* I don't know, I can't see Juan's lantern any longer.

JOSÉ *sulkily:* Don't tell me it just vanished.

THE MOTHER: No, it's really gone.

José goes to the window, looks out.

JOSÉ *with a strange voice to the worker:* Yes, it's gone! Last time he was way out at the Cape. I'm running down. *He runs out quickly.*

THE WORKER: He may be on his way back.

THE MOTHER: We'd still see his light.

THE WORKER: What could have happened?

THE MOTHER: I know what's happened. She's rowed out to meet him.

THE WORKER: Who? The girl? Not her!

THE MOTHER: I'm sure they went out to get him. *With mounting agitation:* It was a plot. They planned it before-hand. They went on sending one visitor after another all evening so I wouldn't be able to keep watch. They're murderers! The whole lot of them!

THE WORKER *half joking, half angry:* Don't tell me they sent the priest.

THE MOTHER: They won't stop till they've dragged every-one in.

THE WORKER: You mean he's made off for the front?

THE MOTHER: They're his murderers, but he's no better than they are. Sneaking off at night. I never want to see him again.

THE WORKER: I just don't understand you any more, Teresa. Can't you see there's nothing worse you can do to him now than hold him back from fighting? He won't thank you for it.

THE MOTHER *absently:* It wasn't for my sake I told him not to fight.

THE WORKER: You can't call it not fighting, Teresa; when he's not fighting on our side, he's fighting for the generals.

THE MOTHER: If he has done this to me and joined the militia I'm going to curse him. Let them hit him with their bombs! Let them crush him with their tanks! To show him that you can't make a mockery of God. And that a poor man can't beat the generals. I didn't bring him into the world to ambush his fellow men behind a machine gun. Maybe there has to be injustice in this world, but I didn't teach him to take part in it. When he comes back telling me he's defeated the generals, it's not going to make me open the door to him. I'll tell him from behind the door that I won't have a man in my house who has stained himself with blood. I'll cut him off like a bad leg. I will. I've already had one brought back to me. He too thought luck would be on his side. But there's no luck for us. Maybe that will dawn on you all before the generals are through with us. They that take the sword shall perish with the sword.

Murmuring is heard outside the door, then the door opens and three women come in, hands folded over their breasts, murmuring an Ave Maria. They line up along the wall. Through the open door two fishermen carry the dead body of Juan Carrar on a blood-soaked sailcoth. José, deadly pale, walks behind. He is holding his brother's cap in his hand. The fishermen set the body on the floor. One of them holds Juan's lantern. While the mother sits there petrified and the women pray louder, the fishermen explain to the worker with subdued voices what happened.

FIRST FISHERMAN: It was one of their fishing cutters with machine guns. They gunned him down as they passed him.

THE MOTHER: It can't be! There must be a mistake! He only went fishing!

The fishermen are silent. The mother sinks to the floor, the worker picks her up.

THE WORKER: He won't have felt anything.

The mother kneels down beside the dead body.

THE MOTHER: Juan.

For a while only the murmur of the praying women and the muffled roar of the cannon in the distance are heard.

THE MOTHER: Could you lift him up on the chest?

The worker and the fishermen lift the body, carry it to the rear and place it on the chest. The sailcloth remains on the floor. The prayers of the women grow louder and rise in pitch. The mother takes José by the hand and leads him to the body.

THE WORKER *in front again, to the fishermen:* Was he on his own? No other boats out with him?

FIRST FISHERMAN: No. But he was close to the shore. *He points at the second fisherman.*

SECOND FISHERMAN: They didn't even question him. They just flicked their searchlight over him, and then his lantern fell into the boat.

THE WORKER: They must have seen he was only fishing.

SECOND FISHERMAN: Yes, they must have seen that.

THE WORKER: He didn't call out to them?

SECOND FISHERMAN: I'd have heard.

The mother comes forward, holding Juan's cap which José had brought in.

THE MOTHER *simply:* Blame it on his cap.

FIRST FISHERMAN: What do you mean?

THE MOTHER: It's shabby. Not like a gentleman's.

FIRST FISHERMAN: But they can't just loose off at everybody with a shabby cap.

THE MOTHER: Yes they can. They're not human. They're a canker and they've got to be burned out like a canker. *To the praying women, politely.* I'd like you to leave now. I have a few things to do and, as you see, my brother is with me. *The people leave.*

FIRST FISHERMAN: We've made his boat fast down below.

When they are alone the mother picks up the sailcloth and gazes at it.

THE MOTHER: A minute ago I tore up a flag. Now they've brought me a new one.

She drags the sailcloth to the rear and covers the body with it. At this moment the distant thunder of the guns changes. Suddenly it is coming closer.

JOSÉ *listlessly:* What's that?

THE WORKER, *suddenly looking harassed:* They've broken through! I've got to go!

THE MOTHER, *going to the oven in front, loudly:* Take the guns! Get ready, José! The bread's done too.

While the worker takes the rifles from the box she looks after the bread. She takes it out of the oven, wraps it in a cloth and goes over to the men. She reaches for one of the rifles.

JOSÉ: What, you coming too?

THE MOTHER: Yes, for Juan.

They go to the door.

Notes and Variants
to *Fear and Misery of the Third Reich*

Texts by Brecht

Undoubtedly the sight of Germany, our home country, has today become terrifying to the rest of the world: that is, in so far as the world is bourgeois, to the bourgeois world. Even among the Third Reich's friends there can hardly be one that has never been terrified by Germany as it now is.

Anyone who talks about Germany becomes a diviner of mysteries. One favourite interpretation of the mystery which we have read on various occasions and in various languages, not excluding our own, goes like this: here is a country at the heart of Europe, a long-established nursery of culture, which was plunged overnight into barbarism, a sudden horrible senseless outbreak of savagery. The forces of good were defeated and the forces of evil got the upper hand.

Such is the interpretation, and it argues that barbarism springs from barbarism. The impetus comes from impulse. The impulse comes from nowhere but was always there. In this interpretation the Third Reich is a natural event, comparable with a volcanic eruption which lays waste fertile land.

The most powerful living English statesman has spoken of the German overestimation of the State. To him, naturally, the State is something natural; once you overestimate it, however, it becomes something unnatural. Think of Schiller's lines:

> Fire is to our benefit
> Only if one watches it

– and the object lesson that follows them.

According to this interpretation a particular unnatural state derives from overestimation of the State. How this overestimation comes about in the first place is left open.

Some interpretations are more realistic: for instance the following. Germany is a great state and industrially very strong. It has to make sure that it gets provided with markets and sources of raw materials. Twenty years ago it fought for markets and raw materials and was defeated. The victors hamstrung the State as such while promoting still further expansion of its industry by means of loan aid. Its industry's former markets and raw material reserves were never enough and now they had been partly taken away. No wonder that industry got the State functioning again. The State will have another shot at the old objectives.

People who talk that way at least have some explanation for the German 'overestimation' of the State, but even they have no explanation for the barbarism prevalent in Germany short of saying yet again that it springs from barbarism. Perhaps they see that state as an ordinary state which has got into an exceptional situation and therefore must have recourse to exceptional means; all the same the means inevitably terrify them.

For these exceptional means clearly have something of the character of malignant growths. They can't just be explained away by the exceptional situation.

This is why such people find the persecution of the Jews, for instance, so exasperating, because it seems such an 'unnecessary' excess. They regard it as something extraneous, irrelevant to the business in hand. In their view pogroms are not esssential to the conquest of markets and raw materials, and accordingly can be dispensed with.

They fail to understand that barbarism in Germany is a consequence of class conflicts, and so they cannot grasp the Fascist principle which demands that class conflicts be converted into race conflicts. They can keep their parliaments, because they have parliamentary majorities.

But the bourgeois world is profoundly reluctant to look and see what exceptional means a state can employ to master exceptional situations; what's more, virtually all rules were at one time exceptions. Is it really possible that culture might become the ballast that has to be jettisoned so that this particular balloon may rise?

The same powerful English statesman who regretted the German tendency to overestimate the State was voicing this reluctance when he spoke of conditions under which life would no longer be worth while. Does it ever strike him that there are also 'natural' states to whose inhabitants the same thing applies?

Germany, our home, has transformed itself into a people of two million spies and eighty million people being spied on. Life for these people consists in the case being made against them. They are made up exclusively of the guilty.

When the father says something to his son it is to avoid being arrested. The priest thumbs through his Bible to find sentences he can quote without being arrested. The teacher puzzles over some action of Charlemagne's looking for motives that he can teach without somebody arresting him. The doctor who signs a death certificate chooses a cause of death that is not going to lead to his arrest. The poet racks his brains for a rhyme he won't be arrested for. And it is to escape arrest that the farmer decides not to feed his sow.

As you can see, the measures which the State is driven to take are exceptional.

The bourgeois world desperately seeks to prove that the State is making a mistake, that it is not forced to take them; that force may be necessary (what with the exceptional circumstances), but not all that much force, just so much force and no more; that moderate punishment is enough; that occasional spying will suffice; that military preparations within rational limits are to be preferred.

And the bourgeois world has a vague feeling that it is wrong. This question of the degree of compulsion necessary in Germany is preoccupying the bourgeoisie of many nations, including the German. The way the German upper bourgeoisie saw it was this: large scale property-owning had to be maintained, and the deal was 'by whatever means'. The State was massively built up. There are now supposed to be odd pockets of incomprehension among the upper bourgeoisie, restrictions placed on the means. All of a sudden it's no longer supposed to be by whatever means, just by some. Grumbling can be heard.

Now and then a head rolls, and now and then the odd grumble is heard. 'That signifies discontent,' say those who have fled. Does it? Does a 27-year-old student mother have to be beheaded for the same reason that the Rhineland industrialists' memorandum had to be torn up? If this really is discontent, just tell me how much.

Has the regime outstayed its welcome, does it really 'represent nobody but itself'?

The expression 'discontent rules' is not a happy one. Discontent does anything but rule. The regime is a foreign body? But the knife in a bandit's hand is a foreign body too. The industrialists are having to be kept down now? Down on top of what? Of the workers? The loss of freedom affects all alike? Does this mean that all wish all to be free?

The regime forces the workers to submit to exploitation and accordingly strips them of their trade unions, parties, newspapers.

The regime forces the employers to exploit the workers, lays down specific forms of exploitation, makes it conform to plan and foists General Goering on the employers, hence the unfreedom felt 'on all sides'.

The regime's great strength, it is said, lies in the absence of any sign of opposition. This can't apply to the workers; now and then a head rolls. It can apply to the bourgeoisie, even though now and then the odd grumble is heard. Such grumbles are not an opposition.

Admittedly that leaves the great middle class, the mass of petty bourgeoisie and peasantry. Of every ten of these people two can be seen as holding down the other eight. For them the great question, what degree of culturally destructive means should be tolerated so that the regime can maintain large-scale ownership, boils down to this: is small-scale ownership dependent on large? Certain groups get some marginal droppings from the loot, or hope to do so. Others have been unable to see the difference between their own possessions and possession of the means of production. Anyhow they aren't asked.

Whoever clings to cultural concepts will get arrested. In the great war which will shortly have to be authorised for the maintenance of large-scale ownership, those who cling to life (which is also a cultural value) will be punished by death. This fear is beginning to overshadow all others.

The regime and the middle orders confront one another in a frenzied bargaining process. The regime is brandishing a list of luxuries due to be sacrificed for the maintenance of ownership. The middle orders are haggling. 'All right, scrap Goethe. But can't we keep religion?' – 'No.' – 'Surely a little freedom of opinion can't do any harm?' – 'Yes it can.' – 'But our children, can't we . . .?' – 'What are you thinking of?' – 'Our bare life?' – 'Will have to be committed.'

The thought that barbarism springs from barbarism won't help solve the dreadful problem of Germany. The degree of violence employed implies the degree of opposition: to that extent the acts of violence are due not to spontaneous impulses but to deliberate reckoning, and have a touch of rationality however much stupidity, ambiguity and miscalculation may also be involved. But just as the oppression is of varying kinds, so also is the opposition. Those sections of the people who are now nervously asking '*how many* culturally destructive means are really needed to maintain large-scale ownership of capital, land and machinery?' probably get a truthful answer from the regime when it bellows back 'Just as many as we are using.' Might the sections in question have to be forced into the same condition of extreme dehumanisation that the proletariat, according to the Socialist classics, is resisting by its fight for the dignity of mankind? Will it be the misery that eventually defeats the fear?

[GW 20, pp. 246–251. Unpublished in Brecht's lifetime. The 'British statesman' referred to appears to be Neville Chamberlain, who became P.M. in May 1937. See the short note 'Mr Chamberlain's Dream' which precedes this in *GW* and duplicates certain of its arguments.]

NOTE TO *Fear and Misery of the Third Reich*

The play 'Fear and Misery of the Third Reich' offers the actor more temptation to use an acting method appropriate to a dramaturgically Aristotelian play than do other plays in this collection. To allow it to be performed immediately, under the unfavourable circumstances of exile, it is written in such a way that it can be performed by tiny theatre groups (the existing workers' groups) and in a partial selection (based on a given choice of individual scenes). The workers' groups are neither capable nor desirous of conjuring up the spectators' empathetic feeling: the few professionals at their disposal are versed in the epic method of acting which they learnt from the theatrical experiments of the decade prior to the fascist regime. The acting methods of these professionals accord admirably with those of the workers' groups. Those theorists who have recently taken to treating the *montage* technique as a purely formal principle are hereby confronted with montage as a practical matter, and this may make them shift their speculations back to solid ground.

[GW 15, p. 1099. Possibly intended for the Malik–Verlag edition. The last sentence is aimed at George Lukács.]

FURTHER NOTE

The cycle 'Fear and Misery of the Third Reich' is a documentary play. Censorship problems and material difficulties have hitherto prevented the available small workers' theatre groups from performing more than a few isolated scenes, using simple indications of scenery (for instance, playing against dimly lit swastika flags).

Given a revolving or a multiple set however, almost any theatre could resolve the play's technical problems; anyhow, it should be feasible to stage a selection of 17 scenes (1, 2, 5, 6, 7, 8, 9, 12, 13, 16, 18, 19, 20, 22, 23, 25, 27). The play shows behaviour patterns typical of people of different classes under Fascist dictatorship, and not only the gests of caution, self-protection, alarm and so forth but also that of resistance need to be brought out. In the series of VERSUCHE whose publication began in 1930 this play constitutes no. 20.

[BBA 1156/83. May also have been intended for the Malik publication, which was interrupted in 1938/39.]

NOTES TO *Fear and Misery of the Third Reich*

'Fear and Misery of the Third Reich' derives from eyewitness accounts and press reports.

The Malik–Verlag had these scenes printed in Prague in 1938, but distribution was prevented by Hitler's invasion.

A stage version for America was performed in New York under the title 'The Private Life of the Master Race'. This comprises:

in part I, scenes 2, 3, 4, 13 and 14
in part II, scenes 8, 9, 6 and 10
in part III, scenes 15, 19, 17, 11, 18, 16, 20 and 24.

The basic constituent of the set is the classic armoured troop-carrier of the Nazi army. This appears four times, at the beginning, between the parts and at the end. The individual scenes are separated by a voice and by the rumbling of the troop-carrier. This rumbling also becomes audible during the scenes, at the onset of the terror which the carrier's crew bring with them.

For instance:

Part I. To the sound of a barbaric military march a large signpost looms out of the darkness bearing the inscription 'TO POLAND' and with the troop carrier beside it. This is manned by 12–16 soldiers with rifles between their knees, steel helmets and chalk-white faces. Thereupon:

CHORUS: Now that the Führer . . .
              . . . by his steelhard hand.

The scene grows dark again. The dull rumble of the waggon

continues for a few seconds. Then the lights go up and a
landing is seen. Over the stage are suspended big black letters:
BRESLAU, SCHUSTERGASSE 2. This is followed by scene 2.
Thereupon:

VOICE: *'That's how neighbour . . .*
       . . . taken on to our waggon.'

CHORUS IN THE ARMOURED TROOP-CARRIER

Before Part I:

> Now that the Führer has created order
> In his own country with his steely hand
> He's made us take up arms and drive across the border
> To do the same in every neighbouring land.
> So we set out as told by our superiors
> With all our might – it was a summer day –
> And launched a blitzkrieg on those German-peopled areas
> Whose ancient towns were under Polish sway.
> Scarlet with blood, our tanks rolled ever faster
> Right from the Seine to Volga's ice strand.
> Thanks to the Führer the world must acknowledge us as a
> Race, forged for ever by his steely hand.   [master-

Before Part II:

> Treason and discord split the world we live in
> And all the time our tank accelerates:
> Their discord hoists white flags to show they give in
> Their treason now will help us force the gates.
> They saw our tank roll on its sacred mission
> To Denmark's shores through fields of blue-green flax.
> Those peoples who deny the Führer's vision
> Will soon be crushed beneath our rumbling tracks.
> For what he's done for our own German nation
> He's going to do for Europe as a whole
> Iceland to Italy will be one vast plantation
> Of our New Order's swastika symbol.

Before Part III:

> You see, our tank was made by Krupp von Bohlen
> And three old bankers played a useful part

And then von Thyssen made it tracks to roll on
Twelve big proprietors gave it a good start.

After Part III:

But after two more winters making war
We found our tanks began to show the strain
Until we got cold feet because we'd come too far
And felt we'd never see our home again

We pressed on east across each conquered land till
Fresh snow clogged up the crown our Führer wore
And then at last our tanks came to a total standstill
Once we had reached the country of the poor.

Thus we went forth to impose the chains that bind us
And, violated, turned to violence.
Now we see death in front of us and death behind us.
Our homes are far away, the cold intense.

THE VOICE

After scene 2:

That's how neighbour betrayed his neighbour
How the little people ripped one another apart
And enmity grew in tenements and city districts
And we strode in confidently
And took on to our battle waggon
All who had not been beaten to death:
This whole people of betrayers and betrayed
Was taken on to our waggon.

After scene 3:

From factories and kitchens and labour exchanges
We collected a crew for our waggon.
Paupers dragged paupers to our waggon.
With the kiss of Judas we took him on our waggon
With a friendly pat on the shoulder
We took them on our battle waggon.

After scene 4:

> The people's disunity gave us our greatness.
> Our prisoners still fought each other in the concentration
>   camps
> Then they all ended up on our waggon.
> The prisoners came on our waggon
> Tormentors and tormented
> The whole lot came on our battle waggon.

After scene 13:

> We covered the good worker with approval
> And heaped him high with menaces.
> We put flower boxes round the sweatshop he worked in
> And SS men at the exit.
> With salvoes of applause and salvoes of rifle fire
> We loaded him on our battle waggon.

Before scene 8:

> Pressing their children closer
> Mothers in Britanny stand and humbly search
> The skies for the inventions of our learned men.
> For there are learned men too on our waggon
> Pupils of the notorious Einstein
> First given an iron schooling by the Fuhrer
> And taught what Aryan science is.

Before scene 9:

> A doctor too is on our waggon
> He decides which Polish miners' wives
> Shall be sent off to the brothel in Krakow
> And he does this well and without any fuss
> In memory of the loss of *his* wife
> Who was Jewish and got sent away
> Because a member of the Master Race has to be carefully
>   coupled
> And the Führer decides who he is to lie with.

Before scene 6:

>   And there are also judges on our waggon
>   Adept at taking hostages, picked from a hundred victims
>   Accused of being Frenchmen
>   And found guilty of loving their country
>   For our judges are well versed in German law
>   And know what is demanded of them.

Before scene 10:

>   And there is a teacher too on our waggon
>   A captain now, with a hat of steel
>   Who delivers his lessons
>   To Norway's fishermen and the wine-growers of Champagne
>   For there was a day seven years ago
>   Now faded but never forgotten
>   When in the bosom of his own family he learned
>   Hatred of spies.
>   And whenever we arrived we incited father against son
>   And friend against friend.
>   And the mischief we made in foreign countries was no differ-
>   ent from
>   The mischief we made in our own.

Before scene 19:

>   And there is no other business but ours
>   And nobody knows how long we shall keep it.

Before scene 17:

>   Here we come as hungry as locusts
>   And eat out entire countries in a single week
>   For we were given guns instead of butter
>   And we have long mixed bran with our daily bread.

Before scene 11:

>   And whenever we arrive no mother is safe, and no child
>   For we did not spare
>   Our own children.

Before scene 18:

> And the corn in the barn is not safe from us
> Nor the cattle in the byre
> For our cattle were taken away from us.

Before scene 16:

> And we take away their sons and their daughters
> And toss them potatoes in the goodness of our hearts
> And tell them to shout 'Heil Hitler' like our own mothers
> As if they were skewered.

Before scene 20:

> And there is no god
> But Adolf Hitler.

Before scene 24:

> And we subjugated foreign peoples
> As we have subjugated our own.

ADDITIONAL SCENES

Ersatz feelings

Family of Gnauer the bookbinder. Gnauer is sitting in his SA uniform. It is eight in the evening. The doctor is examining the bookbinder's sick sister in the next room.

THE SON *standing indecisively by the radio:* I wonder if we ought to have the radio just now. Aunt Frieda's so feeble. It might just get her worked up.

THE FATHER: She's always been keen on our national resurgence. She lives for that. Which is more than be said of you. Put it on.

THE SON: I was thinking, what with the doctor being in there.
It'll give him the wrong idea.

THE FATHER: That's a phony excuse. In other words, un-
German. Frieda would never let us miss anything on her account. I'd say Germany's food position was an important
enough matter.

THE MOTHER: You're to put it on.

VOICE ON THE RADIO: Professor Dr Seifner of the Health
Advisory Council will now give a talk on 'The Scientist's view
of the Four-Year Plan with particular regard to the availability
of edible fats'.

ANOTHER VOICE: It is a regrettable if all too familiar fact that
mankind is not always aware what is in its own best interest and
what not. Certain of our national comrades have been known to
judge the comprehensive measures which the government takes
in the interests of the whole people, according to the degree of
sacrifice demanded of the individual judging. This is of course a
very human characteristic. Looked at closely, however, this
presumed sacrifice often turns out to be no sacrifice but an act
of kindness. Thus suppose we take nutrition in the context of
the Four-Year Plan: a certain amount of petty grumbling might
be heard to the effect that there are slight shortages of milk here
and of fat there. Those concerned will be surprised to learn
from science that such a shortage of fat for instance may consti-
tute a positive act of kindness to their body. Recently a committee of scientific experts conducted a thorough investigation
of the way in which the human body reacts to a low-fat diet.
Let us consider the conclusions that this committee of top aca-
demics came to.

*Drying his hands, the doctor enters from the next room. The father
makes a sign to his son, who turns off the radio.*

THE FATHER: What's the verdict, doctor?

THE DOCTOR: Not good. She'll have to have an operation.

THE MOTHER: That's dreadful.

THE DOCTOR: Yes, it's a serious business at her age.

THE MOTHER: We thought it would be all right if she was properly
looked after. That's why we got a nurse in. She isn't cheap.

THE DOCTOR: But now an operation's unavoidable. The tumour's
practically blocked the entrance to her stomach. She'll die if
she's not operated.

THE FATHER: That's a major operation, I suppose.

THE DOCTOR: It is.

THE FATHER: Expensive?

THE DOCTOR: You'd have to reckon somewhere between two and three thousand marks.

THE FATHER: That's rather more than we could manage, you know.

THE MOTHER: Poor Frieda.

THE FATHER: So I must ask you for an absolutely straight answer, Doctor. Will this operation cure my sister?

THE DOCTOR: There's a good chance.

THE FATHER: What do you mean, a good chance? In other words it's not even certain she'll be cured?

THE DOCTOR: I mean that we shall remove the tumour and hope it doesn't return. In other words there's a good chance of a cure and at least she'll gain time.

THE MOTHER: I wonder if that kind of time is much gain. When she's suffering.

THE DOCTOR: Starving to death isn't pleasant either, Mrs Gnauer. If we leave her as she is she'll starve.

THE FATHER: But the tumour might return?

THE DOCTOR: It might.

THE FATHER: So it isn't even certain the operation will cure her.

THE DOCTOR: No, but it's certain she'd die without it.

THE FATHER: Of course.

THE DOCTOR: Yes, of course. Think it over, but don't take too long. Good night.

THE FATHER: Good night, doctor.

The doctor leaves.

THE FATHER: Well, there we are

THE SON: Poor Aunt Frieda.

The daughter stands up, goes to the mirror and prepares to go out.

THE FATHER: Where are you off to?

THE DAUGHTER: We've a lecture. Race and Home.

THE FATHER: You'll have to stay here a moment. I'm due over at the SA myself. But first of all there's a decision to be taken, and I want you all to be present.

THE DAUGHTER *pouting*: What am I supposed to decide?

The nurse enters from the next room.

THE NURSE: Miss Gnauer is asking if Mrs Gnauer would come in for a minute.

THE MOTHER: Yes, I'll come.

The nurse goes back: the mother remains seated.

THE SON: What is there to decide? she's got to be operated.

THE FATHER: Don't be so smart. An operation is no joke.

THE MOTHER: At her age.

THE FATHER: Didn't you hear what the doctor said? About that?

THE SON: He also said she'd die without it.

THE FATHER: And that she might die if she has it.

THE MOTHER: I never realised she was in such a bad way.

THE SON: A very bad way, if you ask me.

THE FATHER *suspiciously*: What d'you mean by that?

THE DAUGHTER: Just another of his mean remarks.

THE MOTHER: Stop quarrelling, you two.

THE FATHER: Any sauce from you and you needn't bother to ask for your next pocket-money.

THE SON: Then I won't be able to cycle to school. My inner tubes are past mending now. And I can't get new ones of real rubber. Just ersatz rubber. Same way school nowadays is ersatz school. And this family's an ersatz family.

THE MOTHER: Hans!

THE FATHER: Right. No more pocket-money. And as for the other thing, I wonder if that quack really knows his business. He isn't exactly brilliant. Or he'd charge more than three marks for a visit.

THE MOTHER: His coat is all coming away at the seams and his shoes are patched.

THE FATHER: Anyway there are better doctors than him. I don't go by what he says.

THE SON: Consult a more expensive one, then.

THE MOTHER: Don't talk to your father like that. A more expensive one wouldn't necessarily be better. Not that the nurse isn't dear enough.

THE FATHER: Even the best of them will never give an unbiassed verdict, because he gets part of the surgeon's fee. It's the usual practice with surgeons.

THE SON: That doctor seemed straight, I thought.

THE FATHER: You thought. I didn't think so at all. And however straight they are, people act in their own interests. I've yet to come across a man who doesn't put his own interests first. What he says may sound all very humanitarian and idealistic, but what he actually thinks is another kettle of fish.

THE MOTHER: So you think the operation mayn't be at all necessary?

THE FATHER: Who can tell?

The nurse again appears at the door.

THE NURSE: Couldn't you come, Mrs Gnauer? My patient's worried on account of the doctor being there.

THE MOTHER: Right, I'm just coming. We've a small matter to discuss. Tell her I'll come at once.

The nurse goes back.

THE FATHER: Take the paper in to her. *The son takes a paper and is about to leave.*

THE FATHER: When'll you learn not to give her today's paper before I've read it?

THE MOTHER: But that's yesterday's. Why do you think I put it on the music stand?

THE SON: But cancer's not infectious.

THE FATHER: It is for me, given that the possibility's not ruled out.

THE MOTHER: The news will be the same anyway. Give her last month's and it'll hardly be any different.

THE SON: Ersatz newspapers. All the same the nurse might notice.

THE FATHER: I'm not paying her to read papers.

The son takes the previous day's newspaper into the next room.

THE FATHER: All I want to say is that it's a great deal of money.

THE MOTHER: What with there being no certainty of a cure.

THE FATHER: Exactly. *Pause.* What she's got in the bank would cover it, but there'd be very little over. Three thousand.

THE MOTHER: It'd be a crime to waste all that money on an uncertain operation. Poor Frieda earned every bit of it penny by penny working as a maidservant.

The son returns.

THE SON: She's pretty scared.

THE FATHER: Did the doctor tell her there was question of an operation?

THE SON: No.

THE FATHER: I wouldn't have put it beyond him to upset her like that.

THE SON: I think she's more scared of what you people are talking about here.

THE FATHER: Well, of course she's upset. She can't help knowing she's ill. What with not being able to eat now.

THE MOTHER: It's a bad business. For us too. There are you, having to work all day and you come back to such misery.

THE SON: Have you made your minds up yet?

THE FATHER: It is a great responsibility.

THE SON: It certainly is.

THE MOTHER: If only it was definite and not just a possibility.

THE FATHER: Definite my foot. It's a pure experiment.

THE MOTHER: When he shrugged his shoulders like that I could tell at once he wasn't sure.

THE FATHER: In fact he made no bones about it. All they want is to make experiments. Won't even let you die in peace. Just cut you open once more and talk about good chances. After which they say 'we tried everything'. You bet, with us paying!

THE MOTHER: Shoving a poor old woman in hospital. Away from her own home surroundings. I don't like that one little bit.

THE FATHER: That's not at all what I'm talking about. If the operation was a sure way of getting her back to health I'd be for it right away. This very night. Nobody would have any right to turn down an operation like that.

THE SON: I wouldn't say we had the right in any case. Because there *is* a good chance and it'd be her own money.

THE FATHER: Who's talking about money? Did I mention money? I'm saying it'd be sheer cruelty to inflict another major operation on my sister after all she's had to go through already. Haven't you got any feelings? How can you speak of money? You should be thoroughly ashamed of yourself.

THE SON: I wouldn't say I had any cause to be ashamed of myself.

THE MOTHER: Hans!

THE FATHER: You haven't got two pence worth of feelings in your makeup. All you think about's that bike of yours. And the fact that you'll have to put up with ersatz rubber. Here's our people fighting for its existence, and you've got your mind on your bike. The Führer's raising an army from nothing while we're ringed round by enemies watching us for the least sign of weakness. The whole people is tightening its belts. Look at me collecting all my old toothpaste tubes for the common good. And you've got your mind on your bike and start grumbling about ersatz. With our people confronting its hour of decision. It's for us to decide now. Are we to come up, or are we to sink irretrievably? I'd like to know who is doing as much for our people as the present government. And who takes his responsibilities as seriously. And then we've got this mob, this band of subhumans, who aren't prepared to sacrifice their miserable selfish selves because they can't see that it's all for their own good. But why am I wasting my time talking to you about it? You're not even prepared to sacrifice one of your inner tubes.

THE SON: I simply said I'd need extra pocket money because ersatz rubber costs more than the real thing.

THE FATHER: That's enough of that. I'm fed up with all your unpatriotic talk. Here's the nation undergoing its biggest moral upsurge since the wars of independence and he talks about pocket-money. It's just that kind of materialism that we have to extirpate root and branch. Go off to your room. I don't want to see you.

The son walks to the door in silence.

THE SON *pausing in the doorway*: It isn't her illness she's scared of, it's you two. *He goes out.*

THE MOTHER *calls after him*: That was horrid of you, Hans.

THE DAUGHTER: I've got to be off to the League of German Maidens, Mother. *By the window:* It doesn't look as if it's going to rain. So I'll be able to wear my new jacket. Or do you think it might? Our uniforms are made of synthetic wool, and every drop of rain leaves a mark.

THE MOTHER: Don't you budge.

The nurse appears in the doorway.

THE NURSE: I don't want to disturb you, but my patient is getting into a state. She'd like to talk to one of her family.

THE FATHER: Tell her we'll all come in as soon as we've finished discussing a domestic matter.

The nurse goes back in.

THE FATHER: Not a pleasant character. She's a luxury. What does Frieda need a nurse for? You couldn't ask for anyone less demanding.

THE MOTHER: You wanted to save hospital expenses. And after she was sick that last time who could say it'd be more than a matter of days?

THE FATHER: If I were prepared to take the responsibility for it I'd much sooner hand the whole business over to the doctors. This way I'm just worrying myself to death.

THE MOTHER: In that case they'd surely operate.

THE FATHER: Definitely.

THE MOTHER: Poor Frieda. Getting lugged out of her quiet cosy room yet again.

THE FATHER: Who says I've got anything against operations? Let her have herself cut open as often as she wants: it's up to her.

THE MOTHER: You shouldn't say that. After all, she's your sister. We have to do what's best for her.

THE FATHER: How am I to tell that? Maybe they should operate. I'm not having people say I let my sister starve to death. All I can do is point out that anyone after a major operation like that isn't going to find eating much fun. When nothing's healed up yet.

THE MOTHER: For heaven's sake. Pain with every mouthful. This way at least she won't notice and will just gently flicker out into the beyond.

THE FATHER: You people do as you like. But if they operate and tell you 'it's been cut out but nothing's changed from before', just don't turn on me. It's my considered opinion that when one's ill one has every right to a bit of peace and quiet.

THE MOTHER: Fancy Frieda in hospital. When she's used to having all of us around.

THE FATHER: Here she's with her family. Everything in its accustomed place. She gets looked after. But put her in hospital if you like. Why should I mind?

THE MOTHER: Whoever's suggesting that? Nobody wants her put away. After all she eats like a bird.

THE FATHER: You may find it too much work.

THE MOTHER: No question of that. Frieda's so sensible.

THE FATHER: If you're to be tied because of her . . .

THE MOTHER: We really would miss her. She gave Lotte her new jacket. And then there's her pension too.

THE FATHER: If you ask *me* it'd be in her own best interest to have no more excitements, not: yet another doctor, yet another move, yet more new faces. And if money really has to come into it, then let me point out that the monstrous sum such an operation would cost would be just enough for us to buy that shop in the Möschstrasse for a knockdown price, what with Kott and Sons having gone bankrupt as a Jewish-owned business. That's a bargain that won't occur twice.

THE MOTHER: Did you see their lawyers?

THE FATHER: Without committing us to anything. But of course that shouldn't enter into it. It's Frieda's money.

THE MOTHER: Of course.

THE FATHER: I don't want to be told afterwards that there was anything we failed to do for Frieda.

THE MOTHER: How could they say that? We're doing absolutely everything.

THE FATHER: People are mean enough. You heard how your own son talked.

THE MOTHER: It's really only for Frieda's sake that we're against an operation.

THE FATHER: We can't keep her waiting indefinitely. Of course she's worked up, what with the doctor having been. She'll imagine we're talking about her.

THE MOTHER: In that case I'll tell her . . .
She gets up.

THE FATHER: That the doctor decided there need be no question of an operation.

THE MOTHER: And she needn't worry.

THE FATHER: And that we have gone into it all most conscientiously and decided that it's in her own best interest to stay resting here peacefully rather than go into a nursing home.

THE MOTHER: Where she'd be surrounded by a lot of strangers who wouldn't bother about her.
She goes into the next room. The father turns the radio on once more.

VOICE ON THE RADIO: Accordingly the committee established that too much fat was commonly being eaten. There is no need to consider special measures to counter the fat shortage. In the words of its report, 'we have examined the problem more carefully and conscientiously and come to the conclusion that there is no call for the population to worry since its present diet is not merely adequate but actually much healthier than in the past. Statistics teach us that the effects of a low-fat diet are far from harmful. On the contrary, the human organism is incapable of tolerating as much fat as is generally supposed. We would merely cite the example of China and Japan, where the greater part of the people keeps in excellent health on the plainest diet of rice. Too fatty a diet is more likely to cause disease. A low fat diet guarantees greater energy and longer life. It is not for nothing that the worker is better fitted for physical effort than the so-called intellectual. His supposedly inferior diet is in reality the better of the two. Thus even if our economic situation and lack of colonies did not force our people to save on fat and apply its resources in other ways we are honestly convinced that it would be in its own best interest to do with less fat.

The Internationale

>   Enter the hangmen and floggers
>   The sadists and the sloggers
>   From their war on the 'inner front'.
>   Their arms are tired of flaying
>   And one of them keeps saying
>   'What's the point of this bloody stunt?'

Yard in a concentration camp. Prisoners and SS. A prisoner is being flogged.

THE SS MAN: My arm's hurting. Are you or aren't you going to sing us another verse of that Internationale of yours, you pig?
The prisoner groans under the lash.

THE SS MAN: What about you sods showing how angry you feel when you hear a pig like this singing the Internationale? *To a prisoner:* Hey, you, comrade, take this whip and beat him, but good and hard or it'll be your turn next.
The prisoner in question hesitates.

THE SS MAN: Stubborn, eh?
He hits him. The second prisoner takes the whip and flogs the first.

THE SS MAN: I said good and hard. Ten strokes for you for disobeying orders.
The second prisoner beats harder.

THE SS MAN: Another ten strokes for you, that's twenty in all.
The second prisoner beats harder still. The first prisoner starts singing the Internationale in a hoarse voice. The second stops beating and joins in the song.
The SS men fall on the prisoners.

The Vote

>   With well-armed thugs to lead them
>   And nothing much to feed them
>   Their groans rose to the sky.
>   We asked them, all unknowing:
>   Poor things, where are you going?
>   They said 'to victory'.

29th March 1936. Polling booth. One wall with a big banner: THE
GERMAN PEOPLE NEEDS LIVING SPACE: (ADOLF HITLER).
*SA men standing around. Likewise the official in charge is in SA uniform.
Enter an old woman and a blind man of about forty, escorted by two SA
men. They are very poorly clothed.*

GUARD *announces:* WAR VICTIM!
   All rise and give the Nazi salute.
SA MAN *who has been to collect the pair:* Jakob Kehrer, 34 Rummelsburger Allee, and his mother Mrs Anna Kehrer.
   The pair are given slips and envelopes.
THE OLD WOMAN *to the civilians present:* Do you think there'll be
   another war now?
   Nobody answers. An SA man coughs.
THE OFFICIAL IN CHARGE *to the old woman:* Just show your
   son where to put the cross. *To the SA men, but also addressed
   to the waiting electors:* This man was blinded in the war. But he
   knows where to put his cross. There are plenty of comrades
   can learn from him. This man gladly and joyfully gave his
   eyesight for the nation. But now on hearing his Führer's call
   he has no hesitation about giving his vote once again for Germany's honour. His loyalty to our nation has brought him
   neither possessions nor money. You need only look at his coat
   to see that. Many a habitual grumbler among our comrades
   would do well to think what has led such a man to the poll.
   He points the old woman to the booth: Step in. *The old woman hesitantly guides her blind son to the booth. At one moment she stops
   mistrustfully and looks around. All the SA men are staring at her.
   She is clearly frightened. And shyly, looking back over her shoulder,
   she draws the blind man into the booth.*

The New Dress

   Look: clothes whose classy labels
   Don't say how they're unable
   To stand the slightest rain.
   For they're made of wood and paper
   The wool has been saved for later
   For German troops in Spain.

Hall of a building. It is raining. Two SA men are standing there. Enter a couple who are taking shelter from the rain.

THE MAN: Just a few specks. It'll stop in a moment.

THE GIRL: Look at my dress. A few drops, and just look at my dress. And it cost 28 Marks. Now it's a bit of old rag. Made in Germany. Two drops of rain and just one rag. Who do they think they are, treating a wage-earner that way? 22 Marks a week I get.

THE MAN: Pipe down.

THE GIRL: But you bet the wool goes for uniforms. And we'll soon be left naked. It's a bloody fraud, I saved up for three months. Gave up coffee. Nobody can make that up to me. They're a load of . . .

ONE OF THE SA MEN: Well, Miss?

The girl notices the SA men and gives a scream.

THE MAN: She's just a bit worked up about her dress.

THE GIRL *stammers*: I only meant it shouldn't rain, should it?

Any good against gas?

They come with rubber nozzles
And masks with perspex goggles
Forceps and sterile gauze.
They know that gas is fatal
It's a part of modern battle
And of aggressive wars.

Working-class flat. A worn-out woman and her brother, a worker. It is evening.

THE WOMAN: Potatoes have gone up again.

THE BROTHER: They'll go higher.

THE WOMAN: If they've got nothing for folk to eat they can't make war.

THE BROTHER: Wrong. They can't make war if they got nothing for folk to eat, but then they'll have to make war.

THE WOMAN: I'm having trouble with the boy 'cause he won't stop talking about war, don't you do the same.

THE BROTHER: How's the girl?

THE WOMAN: She's coughing.

THE BROTHER: Seen the doctor, has she?

THE WOMAN: Yes.

THE BROTHER: What d'he say?

THE WOMAN: She needs proper food. *The brother laughs*

THE WOMAN: That's nothing to laugh about.

THE BROTHER: What's your husband say about it?

THE WOMAN: Nothing.

THE BROTHER: See anything of the Minzers these days?

THE WOMAN: No, What's there to talk about?

THE BROTHER: Plenty, I'd have thought.

THE WOMAN: But you can't talk about that. As you know.

THE BROTHER: There are people beginning to talk again. And the fewer potatoes there are the more talking they'll do.

THE WOMAN: But you were saying there'd be a war.

THE BROTHER: Someone at the door.

> *The woman leaves the cooker, and goes and opens the door. She recoils. In the doorway stand three Hitler Youth members wearing gas masks.*

THE BROTHER: What sort of a bad joke is this?

THE THREE: Heil Hitler!

THE WOMAN: What d'you want?

THE THREE: Heil Hitler!

THE WOMAN: Paul's not here.

THE THREE: Heil Hitler! *One of them takes off his gas-mask.*

THE WOMAN: Paul!

THE BOY: Cos you're always going on about when gas comes. We only wanted to show you we're prepared.

THE WOMAN: *has to sit down:* I didn't recognise you.

> *One boy throws his gasmask on the table as the three say 'Heil Hitler' and go off laughing.*

THE WOMAN: They're already at war.

THE BROTHER: *picking up the gasmask:* A thing like that's no better than papiermaché. That filter'll let anything through. It's rubbish.

THE WOMAN: What'd be the good of telling him? I still got weak knees. I just didn't recognise him.

THE BROTHER: Right, once they get their hooks on anyone he's not a son any longer.

THE WOMAN: But what am I to tell him?

THE BROTHER: That gasmasks are no good against gas.

THE WOMAN: What is then?

THE BROTHER *in an undertone:* I was on the Eastern front in 1917. The fellows in the trenches opposite did something that

was. They threw out their government. That was the only thing
that was any good, and it was the first time in the history of the
world that anyone did it.

THE WOMAN: You know how thin these walls are.

THE BROTHER: Bloody muzzle! *He throws the gasmask into the
corner.* We'll stay muzzled till we're forced to open our mouths:
once the gas is there.

*There is a ring. The woman quickly and anxiously rises and picks up the
gasmask from the floor.*

Editorial notes

There is no trace of any structural scheme for this work, whose
scenes were individually conceived, arranged in different orders at
different times, and eventually published in what seems to have
been conceived as chronological order, following the dates given
in the initial stage directions. The nucleus evidently consisted of
five scenes – 1. The spy. 2. The Jewish Wife. 3. A matter of
justice. 4. Occupational Disease. 5. The Chalk Cross – under the
overall title *Die Angst (Fear): and subtitled Spiritual Upsurge of the
German People under Nazi Domination.* This was dated 20th–24th
August 1937 by Brecht's collaborator Margarete Steffin. Three
months later Brecht told Karl Korsch that he had written seven.
By the spring of 1938 the number had grown to seventeen, at
which point Brecht added the introductory 'March-past' poem and
had copies made which he sent to Piscator, Dudow and no doubt
others. He described this to Piscator as a 'cycle of very short plays
which might for performance purposes be called *German March-
past*' but had the overall title *Fear and Misery of the Third Reich.*
Scenes in our text which were not included in this first full script
were 2, 4, 11, 12, 13, 14, 20 and 22.

This was the script used for 99%, the version performed that
May in Paris under Dudow's direction, though only eight of its
scenes were played.

But Brecht had evidently got the bit between his teeth, and he
sent Dudow a number of additional scenes till by late May the
total had risen to 27. This was the number included in the new
duplicated script which served as a basis for the unrealised third
volume of the Malik–Verlag edition of Brecht's works, where the

play was to be entitled *Germany – an atrocity story*; this went for type-setting in August 1938. A copy also went to Ferdinand Reyher who spent the first half of 1939 making a first American adaptation. At some point too Brecht sent (or took) the play to Mezhdunarodnaya Kniga in Moscow, who, following the German invasion in 1941, published a selection of thirteen scenes – 1, 2, 5, 7, 10, 13, 14, 16, 18, 19, 22, 23 and 'The Vote' – oddly enough omitting 'The Jewish Wife' and 'The Chalk Cross'.

The wartime *The Private Life of the Master Race* version was originally made in May 1942 in Geman for Max Reinhardt, and now only survives in its translation by Eric Bentley. It is composed of 17 scenes divided into three parts, as detailed in the note on p. 132, with new introductory verses for the different parts and scenes. When in 1945 the Aurora–Verlag (successor to the Malik–Verlag) at last published a full German text – the 24-scene basis for the subsequent Gesammelte Werke and for our own translation – it restored the pre-war verses and loose chronological form, relegating the wartime version to Brecht's note. For the first time it included 'Peat-Bog Soldiers', while five scenes from one or other of the earlier versions were omitted: 'Ersatz Feelings', 'The Vote', 'The New Dress' and 'Any use against gas?'

In the notes on all 29 scenes which follow, the 17 scene script of spring 1938 is referred to as '17 sc.', the duplicated 27 scene script as '27 sc.', '*The Private Life of the Master Race*' as '*PLMR*'. The complete set of Brecht's working scripts, including scenes later omitted, is referred to by its archive number, BBA 420. The main early productions are referred to as '99%' (Dudow, 1938), '1942 production' (Viertel, New York 1942 in German) and '1945 production' (*Private Life of the Master Race*, New York 1945, initiated by Piscator and finally directed by Viertel).

*   *   *

Prologue. The German march-past. *Der Deutsche Heerschau*. Was included, along with the introductory verses to the individual scenes, in *99%*. In the 1945 productions and in *PLMR* it was replaced by the verses on pp. 133–134.

1. One big family. *Volksgemeinschaft*. (First in 17 sc.)
   Much shorter in BBA 420, which starts approximately with the same stage direction, but goes on:

   THE FIRST: What I say is once we're one big family we can go on and make war. They'll scatter like crap off a

> boot when we come along, one solid People of brothers.
> Our mission is to . . . *He stops, freezes and listens. Somewhere*
> *a window has been opened.*
> THE SECOND: Wozzat?

Continuing roughly as on page 6 except for the omission of
THE SECOND's last exclamation.

2. A Case of Betrayal. *Der Verrat*. (First in 27 sc.)
Included in 1945 production and *PLMR*. Derived primarily
from the poem 'The Neighbour' of 1934 (GW 9 p. 515), which,
so far as we know, has not previously been translated:

> I am the neighbour. I reported him.
> None of us want
> Agitators in our building.
>
> When we put out the swastika flag
> He put out nothing.
> Then when we tackled him about it
> He asked if our living room –
> Lived in by us and our 4 children –
> Had enough space for a flagpole
> When we told him we'd believe in the future once more
> He laughed.
>
> When they beat him up on the staircase
> We didn't like that. They ripped his shirt.
> That wasn't necessary. Our kind aren't
> All that well off for shirts.
>
> Still, at least we're rid of him now, and the house is quiet.
> We've plenty to worry about, so
> Quiet at least is essential.
> We've begun to notice one or two people
> Looking away when we run into them. But
> Those who came for him tell us
> We did the right thing.

3. The Chalk Cross. *Das Kreidekreuz*. (In *Die Angst*.)
Dated 18–20. viii 37 by Margarete Steffin in BBA 420. Basked
on poem of 1934 with the same title (Poems 1913–1956, p.
226). Brecht later added the passages (a) from 'THE SA
MAN: That's what women want' . . . to 'We're glad to help'

on p. 9 (b) the SA MAN's three lines as *he puts his hand on hers in a friendly way* on p. 11; and (c) the WORKER's 'Give me the Marxists and the Jews' on p. 13. Included in *99%*, 1942 and 1945 productions and *PLMR* but not in Moscow edition of 1941.

4. Peat-bog soldiers. *Moorsoldaten.*
Presumably written during Brecht's stay in the US. According to Eric Bentley, Elisabeth Hauptmann wrote the closing third, from the SS man's final entrance. The scene was included in 1945 production and *PLMR*. The 'Song of the Peat-bog Soldiers' is an actual concentration camp song.

5. Servants of the people. *Dienst am Volke.* (In 17 Sc.)
Not played in the early productions.

6. A matter of justice. *Rechtsfindung.* (In *Die Angst.*)
Including in *99%*, 1942 and 1944 productions and *PLMR* but not in Moscow edition 1942. Passages added on or after BBA 420 are (a) on pp. 36–7 from '*For some while*' to '*The Judge just looks scared*'. (b) the whole episode with the maidservant from her entrance on p. 37 to her exit on p. 38, (c) the Usher's second appearance on p. 39 from THE SENIOR JUDGE: 'Come in!' to the JUDGE's 'That's something I could have done without' eight lines later, and (d) the concluding seventeen lines following the JUDGE's 'One moment', apart from his final exit.

7. Occupational disease. *Die Berufskrankheit* (In *Die Angst.*)
Included in Moscow edition 1942 but not in *PLMR* or US productions. In BBA 420 the Surgeon originally began with one long speech up to his query 'What has this man got?'; this was subsequently broken up by the exchange with the three Assistants, amplified with medical details (e.g. the naming of Raynaud's Disease) and extensively reworded. His exchanges with the Sister were also added later, as was his 'Why?' and the First Patient's sotto voce question.

8. The Physicists. *Die Physiker.* (In 17 Sc.)
Including in *PLMR*. BBA 420 omits the 5 lines from *grabs for it greedily* on p. 45 to 'Without it we're stuck' and the whole passage read out by Y from 'The problem concerns' (p. 46) to 'remain fixed' (below). Instead it has Y reading '*the whole in-*

comprehensible text with its plethora of formulas in a hushed voice', broken by interruptions as in the final stage-directions. It seems likely that the 'Mikovsky' referred to is an error for (Rudolph) Minkovsky, the name of an eminent astronomer who emigrated to the US in the 1930s and his uncle (Hermann) who contributed to the general theory of relativity and died in 1909.

9. The Jewish Wife. *Die jüdische Frau.* (In *Die Angst.*)
   Was included in 99%, 1942 and 1945 productions and *PLMR*. Not in the Moscow edition, though a script destined for it is in the Lenin Library. There is a script worked on by Brecht (BBA 415/25–35) which shows that at one point the order of the woman's four telephone calls was different: first to Anna, second to Gertrude, third to the bridge-playing doctor and fourth to Mrs Schöck. After that she made a fifth (promptly deleted) call to an asylum to ask whether equivalent institutions in Holland would take in a Jewish woman without means, and another (likewise deleted) to order a photograph for her husband. Two of her imaginary conversations with the husband were added on the same script: those beginning 'Don't tell me you haven't changed' (p. 49) and 'I never told you' (p. 50).

10. The Spy. *Der Spitzel.* (In *Die Angst.*)
    Dated 18 viii 1937 by Steffin. Published in the Moscow *Internationale Literatur* (Deutsche Blätter) no. 3, March 1938 and (as 'The Informer') in Charles Ashleigh's translation in *New Writing*, London. Included in 1942, 99%, 1942 and 1945 productions and *PLMR*. Relates to poem of c. 1934 'Ich bin der Lehrer' (GW 9 p. 558).

11. The Black Shoes. *Die schwarzen Schuhe.* (In 27-scene version.)
    Also called 'Children's Shoes' (*Die Kinderschuhe*) and *Fleisch für Fleisch* (untranslatable pun on the exchanging of flesh for meat). Included in *PLMR* but not played in main early productions.

12. Labour Service. *Arbeitsdienst.* (In 27-scene version.)
    Written by April 1938. Not included in early productions or *PLMR*. THE STUDENT's final line ended with 'for today', to which the YOUNG WORKER replied simply: 'Wait till we're out of here and I'll give you something to remember'.

13. Workers' Playtime. *Die Stunde des Arbeiters.* (In 27-scene version.)

Was among the six newly written scenes sent to Dudow on 24 April 1938. Included in *PLMR*.

14. The Box. *Die Kiste*. (In 27-scene version.)
    Included in 1945 production and *PLMR*. Due to be played in Viertel's 1942 production but omitted at the last moment.

15. Released. *Der Entlassene*. (In 27-scene version.)
    Included in *PLMR* but not played in early productions.

16. Charity begins at home. *Winterhilfe*. (In 17-scene version.)
    Including in *99%*. 'Winter Aid' was the organised Nazi charity for the poor, for which the SA and others went out collecting.

17. Two bakers. *Zwei Bäcker*. (In 17-scene version.)
    Included in *99%* and *PLMR*.

18. The farmer feeds his sow. *Der Bauer füttert die Sau*. (In 17-scene version.)
    Included in *99%* and *PLMR*.

19. The Old Campaigner. *Der alte Kämpfer*. (In 17-scene version.)
    In *PLMR* but not staged in any early productions.

20. The Sermon on the Mount. *Der Bergpredigt*. (In 27-scene version.)
    Also called 'The Question' or 'The Pastor's Question' '*Die Frage* or *Die Frage des Pfarrers*). Staged in 1945 and included in *PLMR*.

21. The Motto. *Das Mahnwort*. In 27-scene version.)
    In the working script BBA 420, the initial stage direction specifics that it is Hitler's birthday but gives no indication of year and city. Not staged in early productions.

22. The barracks learn that Almeria has been bombarded. *In den Kasernen wird die Beschiessung von Almeria bekannt*. (In 27-scene version.)
    Included in 1942 Moscow edition.

23. Job creation. *Arbeitsbeschaffung*. (In 17-scene version.)
    Also called *Arbeitsbeschaffung 1937*). In *99%* and 1942 Moscow edition, both times as closing scene.

24. Consulting the People. *Volksbefragung*. (In 17-scene version.)
    Also called '*The Missing Man*' (*Der Fehlende* or *Der fehlende Mann*)
    In 1945 production and *PLMR*. 13 March 1938 was the official
    death of the Anschluss with Austria, two days after German
    troops moved into that country. According to Eric Bentley,
    Elisabeth Hauptmann added the references to class at the end.

Epilogue

An unfinished epilogue goes (in approximate translation):

> We'll watch them follow the band till
> The whole lot comes to a standstill –
> A beaten, bogged-down élite.
> We'd laugh till we were crying
> If it weren't for our brothers dying
> To bring about his defeat.
>
> And yet historians tell us
> Of other mighty fellows
> Who came to a sticky end.
> The people had revolted
> Thrown off their chains / ... /

BBA 429/06

Additional scenes

(25) Ersatz Feelings. *Der Gefühlsersatz*.
    This scene is in one of the complete scripts, but is at the back
    of the working script BBA 420. It has no introductory verse,
    though the following epigraph may be meant as the theme for
    one:

> Meanness was always shrouded in a little cloak. But now-
> adays the clock is made of synthetic material.

Evidently the scene was discarded at an early stage.

(26) The Internationale. *Die Internationale*.
    In 17- and 27-scene versions and unpublished Malik–Verlag
    proof. Omitted from the Aurora edition of 1945, possibly
    because of similarities with scene 5, 'Servants of the People'.

(27) The Vote. *Die Wahl.*

In 27-scene version and unpublished Malik–Verlag proof. Omitted from Aurora edition of 1945, and thereafter. 29 March 1936 was the date of the German elections in which 99 per cent of the voters voted Nazi. The Rummelsburger Allee was in a working-class area of Berlin.

(28) The New Dress. *Das neue Kleid.*

In 27-scene and unpublished Malik–Verlag proof. Omitted from Aurora edition of 1945, and thereafter.

(29) Any good against gas? *Was hilft gegen Gas?*

In 17-scene version and unpublished Malik–Verlag proof. Proposed by Brecht for inclusion in 99%, but not staged. Omitted from Aurora edition of 1945, and thereafter.

Sketches and fragments (including some in verse) provide the following hints that Brecht at one time or another planned further scenes:

(a) The prospect of war frightens her less than the warden for her block. (A neighbouring tenant gets mistaken for the warden.)

(b) A posh youth loses 10 pfennigs. (Reproaches.)

(c) A lady gets insulted because of her rings. Her husband: 'Next time besides bringing your gas mask don't forget to wear your gloves.'

(d) When can paterfamilias still sit there in his SA uniform after supper?

$\qquad\qquad\qquad\qquad\qquad$ (a–d, BBA 464/30)

(e) A verse introducing General Goering (BBA 9/10)

(f) A voice introduces the builder of the Atlantic Wall – i.e. probably Albert Speer (98/34)

(g) A verse introduces the hygiene experts (353/6)

(h) Corner of a cellar during an air raid precautions exercise. Seufert, a business manager, is crouching against the wall with his wife and child. They are trying on gas masks. (464/11, with twelve lines of dialogue in which a working-class family enter and are asked to sit on the other side of the cellar; they take no notice.)

(i) A fragment of dialogue in which two concentration camp prisoners, named Rullmann and Lüttge, discuss whether the local Group Leader should be termed a neo-pagan or a freethinker.

Notes and Variants
to *Señora Carrar's Rifles*

Texts by Brecht

NOTE TO *Señora Carrar's Rifles*

The little play was written during the first year of the Spanish Civil War for a German group in Paris. It is Aristotelian (empathy-) drama. The drawbacks of this technique can to some extent be made up for by performing the play together with a documentary film showing the events in Spain, or with a propaganda manifestation of any sort.

[GW II, 1938, p. 397]

ART OR POLITICS?

I understand your question. You see me sitting here and looking out across the Sound, which has nothing warlike about it. So what leads me to concern myself with the struggle of the Spanish people against its generals? But you shouldn't forget why I am sitting here. How can I clear my writing of everything that has so affected my life? And my writing too? For I am sitting here as an exile, and one who has been deprived above all else of his listeners and readers – the people whose language I write in and who moreover are not just the customers for my writings but the objects of my most profound interest. I can only write for people I am interested in. Then imaginative writing becomes just like writing letters. And at present the people in question are being subjected to unspeakable sufferings. How am I to keep that out of my writing? And wherever I look, the moment I see a little way beyond this Sound I see people subjected to sufferings of the same kind. However, if mankind is destroyed there will not be any more art. Stringing beautiful words together is not art. How is art to move people if it is not itself moved by what happens to them? If I harden my heart to people's sufferings how can their hearts be uplifted by what I write? And if I make no effort to find them some way out of their suffering, how are they to find their way into my works? The little play we are talking about deals with an Andalusian fisherman's wife and her fight against the generals. I've tried to show how difficult it is for her to decide to fight them: how only the most extreme necessity makes her take up a rifle. It is an appeal to the oppressed to revolt against their oppressors in the name of humanity. For humanity has to become warlike in times like these if it is not to be wiped out. At the same time it is a letter to the fisherman's wife to assure her that not everybody who speaks the German language is in favour of the generals and is despatching bombs and tanks to her country. This letter I write in the name of many Germans both inside and outside Germany's frontiers. They are the majority of Germans, I am sure.

> [GW SLK pp. 251–2, dated February 1938. On the 14th of that month the play was performed in German under the direction of Brecht and Ruth Berlau in Copenhagen at Borups Hojskøle, with Helene Weigel as Carrar.]

DIFFERENT WAYS OF ACTING
(Weigel and Andreassen as Mrs Carrar)

A comparison of Weigel's and Andreassen's performances in the German and Danish productions of *Señora Carrar's Rifles* leads to some useful conclusions about the principles of the epic theatre. Weigel is a highly qualified professional actress and a communist, Andreassen an amateur and a communist. The two productions involved exactly the same movements and used the same set.

The question of talent is irrelevant, since the acting differences that concern us would also be observable if the degree of talent was more or less equal.

The greater 'impressiveness' which everyone saw in Weigel's performance was attributable to factors other than superior talent.

Both actresses respected epic principles in so far as they largely dispensed with empathy in portraying the character, and by so doing allowed the audience to dispense with it too. The difference lay in the fact that Andreassen made this less interesting than did Weigel.

Unlike Andreassen, Weigel managed by every attitude and every sentence to permit, if not force the audience to take a line – to such an extent that those sitting near me several times expressed their displeasure at the attitude of the fisherman's wife as she argued in favour of neutrality – by continually taking a line herself. Andreassen's way of acting had the audience passively following the story. Carrar's opinions ('you have to be neutral') seemed entirely natural and understandable given her environment and what we had been told of her previous history; she could in effect be no different from what she was. Her change of opinion due to a specific experience (the death of the son she had kept out of the battle, in a battle which neutrality had not eliminated), was understood in the same way. It was like following a piece of natural history wherein one repeatedly acknowledges the laws of nature. Even the detailed contradictions in the character's attitude never emerged: Carrar's neutrality as acted by Weigel was never one hundred per cent complete; she hadn't always favoured neutrality and even now had her reservations about it, her appreciation of her sons' attitude, her traits of bellicosity, her disapproval of the priest's attitude, her traits of compromise and so on. The character Andreassen portrayed was far more passive than Weigel's; things happened *to* her rather than by her agency. Nor did Andreassen show the fighter she eventually becomes as a fighter of a specific, contradictory kind (a fighter for the renunciation of force). Weigel showed a fighter for neutrality being transformed into a fighter for the abolition of fighting.

In other words Andreassen's performance didn't make the story sufficiently interesting, and as a result one missed – as one did not with Weigel – any chance to empathise with the character and participate strongly and effectively in her emotions. One actually missed any use of those hypnotic powers which one is normally able to feel in the theatre. Her noble renunciation of such methods, springing from a natural sense of modesty and a high conception of dignity, became something close to a disadvantage. This way of playing the incidents, as naturally involving no contradictions, seemed to call for another type of acting if interest was to be maintained: the suggestive acting of the old-style theatre.

The lesson for Andreassen, in view of her lack of experience and technique in old- and new-style methods alike – is that there are two ways in which she can develop: she can master the one technique or the other. She has to learn either to make her acting suggestive, to practise empathy and induce it, to mobilise more powerful emotions, or else to define her own attitude to the character portrayed and induce the same attitude in the audience. If she wishes to do the latter, then she must develop to the point of recognition what she now more or less obscurely feels, and find ways of turning this recognition into a recognition by the audience. She must know what she is doing, and show that she knows it. She must not just *be* a proletarian when she acts one, but show

how a proletarian woman differs from a member of the middle or lower middle class. She must be conscious of everything that is special about a proletarian and portray this in a special way.

[GW SzT pp. 1100–103. This refers to the Danish production under Ruth Berlau's direction which opened in Copenhagen on 19 December 1937, as well as to the Swedish two months later.]

DIALOGUE ABOUT AN ACTRESS OF THE EPIC THEATRE

THE ACTOR: I've read what you've written about the epic theatre. And now having seen your little Spanish Civil War play, with the outstanding actress of this new method in the title part, I'm quite frankly astounded. Astounded to find it was proper theatre.

ME: Really?

THE ACTOR: Does it surprise you to heat that what you've written about this new method of acting made me expect something utterly dry, abstract, not to say schoolmasterly?

ME: Not specially. No one likes learning these days.

THE ACTOR: It's not considered entertaining, certainly; but it wasn't only your demand for instruction that led me to expect something very remote from theatre, but also the fact that you seemed to be denying the theatre everything that makes it theatrical.

ME: What, for instance?

THE ACTOR: Illusion. Suspense. Any opportunity to empathise.

ME: And did you feel suspense?

THE ACTOR: Yes.

ME: Did you empathise?

THE ACTOR: Not entirely. No.

ME: Wasn't there any illusion?

THE ACTOR: Not really. No.

ME: But you still thought it was theatre?

THE ACTOR: Yes, I did. That was what astounded me. Don't start crowing, though. It was theatre, but all the same it wasn't anything like as new as I'd expect from what you wrote.

ME: To be as new as that it would have to stop being theatre, I suppose?

THE ACTOR: All I'm saying is that it's not all that difficult to do what you're asking for. Apart from Weigel in the lead part, it was performed by amateurs, simple workers who'd never been on a stage before; and Weigel is a great technician who quite clearly got her training in that ordinary old-style theatre which you keep running down.

ME: You're quite right. The new method results in proper theatre. It allows amateurs to make theatre under certain conditions, so long as they haven't quite mastered the old methods, and it allows professionals to make theatre so long as they have partly forgotten them.

THE ACTOR: Ha. I'd have said Weigel displayed too much technique rather than too little or just enough.

ME: I thought she displayed not just technique but the attitude of a fisherman's wife to the generals too?

THE ACTOR: Certainly she displayed that. But technique as well. I mean, she *wasn't* the fisherman's wife, just acting her.

ME: But she really isn't a fisherman's wife. She really was just acting her. And that's just a fact.

THE ACTOR: Of course; she's an actress. But when she plays a fisherman's wife she has to make you forget that. She showed everything that was remarkable about the fisherman's wife's, but she also showed she was showing it.

ME: I get you. She didn't create any illusion that she *was* the fisherman's wife.

THE ACTOR: She was far too conscious of what was remarkable. You could see she was conscious of it. She actually showed you that she was. But of course a real fisherman's wife isn't conscious of that; she's unconscious, of course, of what's remarkable about her. So if you see a character on stage who is conscious of that, then it plainly won't be a fisherman's wife that you're seeing.

ME: — But an actress. I get you.

THE ACTOR: The only thing lacking was for her to look at the audience at certain points as if to ask 'Well, do you see the sort of person I am?'. I'm sure she had developed a complete technique for sustaining this feeling in the audience, the feeling that she is not what she portrays.

ME: Do you think you could describe such a technique?

THE ACTOR: Suppose she had tacitly thought 'And then the fisherman's wife said' before every sentence, then that sentence would have emerged very much as it did. What I mean is, she was plainly speaking another woman's words.

ME: Perfectly right. And why do you make her say 'said'? Why put it in the past tense?

THE ACTOR: Because it's equally plain that she was re-enacting something that had happened in the past; in other words, the spectator is under no illusion that it's happening now or that he himself is witnessing the original incident.

ME: But the fact is that the spectator is not witnessing an original incident. The fact is that he's not in Spain but in the theatre.

THE ACTOR: But after all, one goes to the theatre to get the illusion of having been in Spain, if that is the play's location. Why else go to the theatre?

ME: Is that an exclamation or a question? I think one can find reasons for going to the theatre without wanting to be under any illusion of being in Spain.

THE ACTOR: If you want to be here in Copenhagen you don't have to go to the theatre and see a play which is set in Spain, do you?

ME: You might as well say that if one wants to be in Copenhagen one doesn't have to go to the theatre and see a play set in Copenhagen, mightn't you?

THE ACTOR: If you don't experience anything in the theatre that you could not equally well experience at home, then you don't have to go there, that's a fact.

[GW SzT pp. 414–417. Incomplete]

PROLOGUE TO SEÑORA CARRAR'S RIFLES

Internment camp for Spanish refugees in Perpignan. Barbed wire separates a couple of French soldiers, one of whom is on guard while the other reads a paper, from three Spaniards: a worker in the uniform of the republican militia, a youth wearing a soldier's cap and a woman sitting motionless on the bare ground leaning against a post.

THE NEWSPAPER READER: It's all come out now about why the Czechoslovakian Republic didn't fight when the Germans invaded. That ex-president of theirs fled to Chicago in the United States, and at last he's talking.

THE SENTRY: And what's he said?

The worker is intrigued and steps up to the wire to listen.

THE NEWSPAPER READER: Here, just listen: that makes the second republic they've polished off this year. Well, the ex-president, he's called Beneš . . .

The worker nods impatiently.

THE NEWSPAPER READER: What, you've heard of him, have you? How come?

THE WORKER: We read all that in our papers last September. We had hopes. If Czechoslovakia had fought . . .

THE NEWSPAPER READER: She didn't, and you know why? She had an alliance with the Soviet Union and when the Germans started making noises this fellow Beneš asked Moscow if the Soviets would come to her aid. They said yes they would. But what happened? The big landowners formed up to Beneš and told him he mustn't accept that aid, and they threatened to revolt if he did. They'd sooner see their country under Prussian jackboots than let the people fight alongside the Soviet Union.

THE SENTRY: Think that's true?

THE NEWSPAPER READER: Of course we can't tell. It's in the paper, so probably it isn't.

THE WORKER: I'd say it was true even though it's in the paper. Our big landowners used foreigners against their own people too.

THE SENTRY: What did they do that for?

THE WORKER: Don't you know? Not even now? That's bad, mate. How they sent the bombers in to make us keep our wooden ploughs? The forces of oppression have their own International.

THE NEWSPAPER READER: So what you're saying is that one people gets attacked from inside, then the big shots throw open the door to let the foreign aggressors in so they can help them, while the other is attacked from outside by foreign aggressors, then the big shots throw open the door and help them attack.

THE WORKER: That's how you have to see it if you've been through what we have.

THE SENTRY: Perhaps it's just no use fighting. The Czechs didn't fight, so of course they were beaten. But you lot fought. Well, you've been beaten too, so what's the point of fighting?

THE NEWSPAPER READER: What you got to say to that?

THE WORKER: Plenty. Your best answer would come from that woman, only she doesn't know your language. She's my sister. She used to live in a small fishing village in Catalonia with her two sons. That boy's the only one she's got left. She asked the same question: What's the point of fighting? She didn't keep on asking it right up to the last moment, but for a very long time she did, almost up to the last moment, and a lot of her sort went on like her asking that question 'What's the point of fighting?' for a very long time, almost up to the last moment. And the fact that they went on asking it for so long was one of the reasons why we got beaten, see, and if one day you find yourself asking the same question as them you'll get beaten too.

THE NEWSPAPER READER: Tell us how it all happened, will you?

THE WORKER: Right, I will. As I said, she was living in a village in Catalonia when the generals and the big landowners began their revolt. She had two sons and kept them out of the fighting for a long time. But one evening . . .

[BBA 167/24–25. This and the Epilogue which follows were evidently written in 1939, following the fall of the Republic.]

EPILOGUE TO *Señora Carrar's Rifles*

The internment camp at Perpignan. The worker on the other side of the barbed wire has finished telling his story. The newspaper reader passes him a cigarette.

THE WORKER: Yes, that's how Maria Carrar went into the fight – even her – against our own generals and against a whole world, of which one part helped to crush us while the other part looked on; and that's how she was defeated. And her rifles once again disappeared beneath some floorboards somewhere.

THE NEWSPAPER READER: Do you suppose they'll be brought out again ever?

THE WORKER: I know they will, because she knows what the fight is about now.

[BBA 167/28a. Clearly goes with the Prologue.]

ANOTHER CASE OF APPLIED DIALECTICS

The little play *Señora Carrar's Rifles*, which B. had based on a one-acter by Synge, was being rehearsed for the Ensemble by a young director, with Carrar being played by Weigel who had played her years before in exile under B's direction. We had to tell B. that the ending, where the fisherman's wife gives her young son and her brother the buried rifles, then goes off to the front with them, did not carry conviction. Weigel herself was unable to say what was wrong. As B. came in she was giving a masterly performance showing how the woman, having grown pious and embittered over the use of force, became increasingly worn down in spirit by the repeated visits and continually renewed arguments of the villagers; likewise how she collapsed when they brought in the body of her son who had been out peacefully fishing. Nonetheless B. too saw that her change of mind was not really credible. We gathered round him and swapped views. 'You could understand it if it was just the effect of all that agitation by her brother and the neighbours,' said one of us, 'but the death of the son is too much.' 'You lay too much store by agitation,' said B., shaking his head. 'Better if it was only the son's death,' said another. 'She'd just collapse,' said B. 'I don't get it,' said Weigel eventually. 'She suffers one blow after another, yet nobody believes they have an effect.' 'Just say that again,' said B. Weigel repeated the sentence. 'It's that one-thing-after-another that weakens it,' said P. We had located the flaw. Weigel had allowed Carrar to flinch under each successive blow and collapse under the heaviest one. Instead she ought to have played the way Carrar steeled herself after each blow had devastated her, then all of a sudden collapsed after the last. 'Yes, that's how I played it in Copenhagen,' said Weigel, surprised, 'and it worked there.' 'Curious,' remarked B. after the rehearsal had confirmed our supposition, 'how a fresh effort is needed every time if the laws of the dialectic are to be respected.'

[GW SzT pp. 890–91. This outwardly impersonal account of Egon Monk's rehearsals for the November 1952 production appears to have been written by Brecht himself. It forms part of his 'Dialectics in the Theatre', for which see *Brecht on Theatre* pp. 281–2.]

Editorial Note

It was in September 1936 that Slatan Dudow wrote to Brecht suggesting that he should write a play about the Spanish Civil War which had just broken out. The work seems to have overlapped with the writing of the first five scenes of *Fear and Misery of the Third Reich*, and it too was typed out and dated 24 August 1937, nearly a year after Dudow's letter. By then Franco's troops had taken Bilbao and Santander and were on their way to conquering the whole north-west corner of the country. Originally the play had been titled *Generals over Bilbao*, which suggests that most of the writing must have been done between 19 April – the date given for the action in one version of the script – and 18 June, when Bilbao itself fell. The title however was not changed to the present one till the scripts were ready, when the location too was altered from the Basque coast to that of Andalucia in the far south.

There are two of Brecht's characteristic outline schemes for this play. One, seemingly the earlier, lists eleven episodes:

1. the brother visiting, the food ships are on the way
2. the conversation over cards
        hunger
3. manuela. theresa goes to tell juan
4. search for rifles
5. the tearing of the flag
6. the priest
7. old mrs perez. the woman in the window
9. where is juan?
10. here is juan
11. three rifles for bilbao

The other, seven-episode scheme slightly changes the order, thus:

1. the brother's visit
2. mistrustful, she catches her brother and her son bent over her dead husband's case of rifles. she tears up the flag in which the rifles are packed
3. the card game
4. where is juan?
5. he that taketh the sword shall perish by the sword
6. here is juan
7. the departure

In the text as typed the names of the mother and her son were Theresa Pasqual and Fernando. Brecht changed them first to Mrs Pasqual and José, then to The Mother and The Boy, as now. On what looks like a final script the present title has been written on the cover, while in the opening stage direction 'Basque' has been amended to 'Andalusian' for the fisherman's house and 'Pasqual' changed to 'Carrar'. The prologue and epilogue (pp. 166–68) suggest that Brecht later thought of Theresa as Maria and shifted the setting up to Catalonia, but these changes were never carried out.

The play's first publication was as a 'Sonderdruck' or advance offprint from the second volume of the collected Malik edition of Brecht's works, which was printed in Prague a bare year before the Nazis moved in. The offprint was dated 1937, the complete volume March 1938. The former was prefaced by Brecht's poem 'The actress in exile' (GW 12 p. 781), which is dedicated to Helene Weigel:

> Now she is making up. In the white cubicle
> She sits hunched on the wretched stool.
> With easy gestures
> She puts on her greasepaint before the mirror.
> Carefully she wipes from her face
> All individuality: the slightest sensation
> Will change it. Now and again
> She lets the noble and delicate shoulders
> Fall forward, as with those who do
> Hard work. She is already wearing the coarse blouse
> With the patched elbow. Her canvas shoes
> Are still on the dressing table.
> When she has finished she
> Asks eagerly if the drum has arrived
> Which is to create the noise of gunfire
> And if the big net is
> Already hanging. Then she stands up, small figure
> Great fighter
> Ready to don the canvas shoes and show
> How an Andalusian fisherman's wife
> Fights the generals.

Glossary

Almeria: Spanish coastal town, shelled by German fleet on 31 May 1937.

Aryan: Of Indo-European origin. Term properly used of languages, but serving in Nazi race theory to denote a superior Nordic-Germanic breed of human.

BDM: League of German Maidens. Nazi girls' organisation.

Brown: Nazi colour. Brown House: party HQ in Munich, cradle of the movement. Brown Shirts: the SA.

Ersatz: Substitute. A term much used of synthetic materials, whose use was forced on the Nazis by economic problems.

Goebbels, Josef: Nazi Propaganda Minister (suicide 1945).

Goering, Hermann: Nazi Economics Minister (suicide 1946).

Kautzky, Karl: Austrian Socialist leader/theorist of Social-Democracy and opponent of Lenin.

Labour Service: Conscripted labour force run on quasi-military lines.

Ley, Dr: Nazi Labour Minister.

Oranienburg: Early concentration camp near Berlin, better known as Sachsenhausen.

Queipo de Llano: Spanish nationalist general. Principal Franco propagandist.

Racial profanation (*Rassenschande*): Sexual relations between Aryans and Jews (or Blacks), prohibited in 1934.

Radio General: Queipo de Llano, q.v.

Scharführer: Nazi paramilitary officer's rank.

Silesia: South-Eastern province of Germany, now partly incorporated into Poland.

Strength through Joy (*Kraft durch Freude*): Nazi travel and leisure organisation, directed to the workers.

Subhumans (*Untermenschen*): Term used of Slavs, Jews, Blacks and other 'non-Aryans'.

Thälmann, Ernst: German Communist Party secretary, imprisoned and executed by the Nazis. Gave his name to German anti-Fascist forces in the Spanish Civil War.

Thyssen: Dynasty of Rhineland heavy industrialists, who flourished before, during and after the above.

United Front: Short-lived Communist policy of alliance with Socialist rank-and-file, c. 1932.

Völkischer Beobachter: Nazi party daily paper.

Winter Aid. Nazi relief organisation, distributing clothing and food parcels to the poor.